Make-Believe

D1477316

ACKNOWLEDGEMENTS

An author's name will appear on the front cover of most books, but no book is the work of a single person. The person whose name is on the cover knows there are more people involved than the named individual. Looking over my shoulders as I have written are more people than I can reasonably name, and some whose names I do not even know because behind this book are many other books. Some are the novels I discuss and, behind them, are people unknown to me. This is a vast circle of writers and readers, to whom I say 'Thank you.' I am also aware that this book is the product of the many conversations I have had with writers, readers, scholars and thinking Christians over many years, and I am grateful for the cumulative effect these have had on me as a person, a reader and a minister. Most of all, I thank my ever-supportive wife, Yvette.

I am grateful to the staff in each department of Lutterworth Press. All have been a pleasure to work with, but I am especially indebted to my copy-editor, Frazer Merritt, who championed this work from the outset and Debora Nicosia who gave it its final look.

Chapter 8 is based on my essay in *The Edinburgh Companion to the Bible and the Arts*, edited by Stephen Prickett (Edinburgh: Edinburgh University Press, 2014), for which I retain copyright. I am grateful to both Stephen and the publishers for giving me the opportunity to begin thinking about this matter.

Permission has been sought for all texts quoted and I have been asked to make the following specific acknowledgements:

Credo: The Apostles' Creed Explained for Today by Hans Küng is © Hans Küng 2000. Published by SCM Press. Used by permission of rights@hymnsam.co.uk.

On Being a Christian by Hans Küng is © Hans Küng 1976. Reprinted by permission of HarperCollins Publishers Ltd.

Chapter 1

MAKING BELIEVE

I will tell you a story to make you believe in God. Not my claim, but that of the narrator of one of the most successful novels of the first two decades of the twenty-first century, Yann Martel's *Life of Pi*. This study of God in twenty-first-century British fiction does not so much assess whether any narrative can convince agnostics and nonbelievers to become theists; rather, it asks why so many contemporary British novelists persist in exploring theological, religious and spiritual themes in their fiction, despite writing in a Britain where suspicion of organised religion prevails. Why is God still in their texts?

The title of this book comes from when I was seven years old. One of my earliest memories in my literary education is of my primary school teacher explaining the difference between fiction and non-fiction in terms a child might understand. She described fiction as 'make-believe'. This is not entirely helpful. Much non-fiction, especially discursive writing, sets out to convince readers to change their minds on matters of opinion and belief, and the notion of make-believe carries a sense of inauthentic 'made-up-ness' and, even, the incredibility of wonderland worlds. And yet, this only applies to a small proportion of fiction. Nevertheless, the notion of stories as make-believe can be comforting: parents settling a child worried that a wolf might come and blow their house down can calm the child's fears by saying the story is only make-believe. I contend that fiction is make-believe, not because it is unreal, but because it has the power to convince. Novels can transport readers to other places, eras and realms, from the material world to transcendence, from tangible reality to the imagined impossible. I have, therefore, often found approaching fiction as make-believe useful and creative in my analysis of novels as a Christian reader. Seeing fiction as make-believe helps us to see the intended status and goal of fiction as narratives bearing truth, however their authors perceive that truth. Martel's *Life of Pi* persuaded very few readers to become believers in God, but the narrative bore truths that enlightened many on the nature of humanity and had much to say about humans as religious beings.

Later in my literary education, I was immersed in eighteenth-century literature. In the provincial grammar school I attended in County Durham, the English Department chose to prepare its A-Level students for the eighteenth-century module. Teachers told us this was because it was the least popular module, and possibly the most difficult, so it increased our chances of impressing markers and achieving better results. We also studied for a general paper, where the most recent text was Thomas Hardy's *Tess of the d'Urbervilles*. I tended, therefore, to see the study of literature as learning the art of writing sentences of Latinate construction. I also saw it as a study, like history, to do with past times. I am, of course, grateful for the opportunity to learn about my language from high Augustan stylists such as Alexander Pope and Samuel Johnson, with their witty linguistic patterns, logical sequences and sonorous amplifications, but my appreciation of beauty and worth in language and literature has since considerably widened. Although lovers of literature can easily be tempted to stay with the classics to appreciate their artistry, turning to the moderns opens up an entirely new world of writing that, often climbing on the shoulders of literary giants of the past, speaks directly to the modern world. Today's fiction is born in today's world and addresses today's world. It both reflects what we see around us and invites changes in what we see there. For this reason, this book fixes strict parameters for itself by discussing only contemporary fiction, by which I mean novels published since the year 2000, and predominantly, and preferably, novels published in the current decade. The writers whose works we discuss in these pages are men and women who live and write in the world as it is now. They tell stories for today's readers.

Unlike much theological writing, this book, despite its title, does not suggest what you should believe. It does not set out orthodoxy for Christian belief. Rather, using fiction as a form of make-believe and a source of God-talk, it invites you to think about why you believe what you believe, and in doing so there may be times when we push at and stretch the boundaries of orthodoxy. Literature provokes readers to imagine God and challenges any theology that is erroneous, thoughtless or unreasonable. To find our way into this study of God in contemporary fiction, we need first to discuss the indispensability of narrative, the roles of story and imagination in theology, the nature of belief, the context in which new novels are written and read, and reading as a social activity.

THE INDISPENSABILITY OF NARRATIVE

Throughout my lifetime, either someone has argued, or it has been the general consensus of opinion, that the novel is exhausted and dying as a literary form. In *The Times Literary Supplement* in 2017, Ben Jeffery said that novels are 'persisting in a kind of zombie state',[1] although each edition of the supplement reviews at least half a dozen newly published works of fiction. Novels, it is often claimed, have been made obsolete by new technology, have fallen out of sync with the values of their surrounding culture and have reached the limits of their capacity to innovate. And yet, the novel still has a pulse. According to some estimates, about 19,000 new novels are published each year in Britain, about eleven per cent of all published books, and the best-selling among them pick up large readerships. Many commuters on Britain's trains, buses and tube continue to make their journeys to and from work bearable with a novel, some on e-books and tablets, but many still in hardback or paperback. I was told when I was young that, as I aged, I would read fewer novels and more non-fiction, perhaps biographies or history books, but that change of life, unlike other anticipated changes, has not happened yet. Fiction – the classics and the newly published – still feeds my thinking, fortifies my work as a church minister and enriches my life. I do my theology, think of God and catch my glimpses of the transcendent world through literature. Perhaps, then, the novel is in better health than the doom-mongers allege. It may be true that, by and large, there is little new in contemporary novels, but every now and again a trailblazer that does something entirely original is published, and many novels, even if not trailblazers, continue to contribute to society's self-awareness by offering both critique of the status quo and opportunities to reform. Often they capture the spirit of the age and hold up a mirror for us to see ourselves as others see us.

Ultimately, novels, or at least something approximating to their form, will not die because narrative is indispensable to the human condition. In 1958, the political philosopher Hannah Arendt published *The Human Condition*, which studied the nature of what she called the active life. In it she discussed our storied selves, saying that every individual life can eventually be told as a story with a beginning and end, and that this is 'the prepolitical and prehistorical condition of history'. History, she said, becomes the storybook of humankind with many actors and speakers, but without identifiable authors, just as each human life tells its story.

1.   24 March 2017, p.7.

Narrative is what results when human consciousness imposes its perceived order onto random and haphazard experience in an effort to make sense of, and find meaning in, existence. Indeed, Ricoeur tells us that past, present and future are not independent, metaphysical entities, but aspects of the human mind's organisational tools that enable us to organise events so that what has happened to us previously is realised in the present as a narrative's plot. In other words, the concepts of past, present and future are human constructs by which we put our experiences into a meaningful storied form. Aristotle called these plots *mythos*, which translates from Greek as myth. For Aristotle, myth was a coherent narrative with beginning, middle and ending imposing order on a series of events. Such myths or plots move from the childish story of 'This happened and then this happened and then this . . .' to a more sophisticated narrative in which cause and effect, point of view, priority and changes of order feature. We cannot fully live without our *mythoi*. We might expect to need to treat these stories with caution, because as the literary scholar Terry Wright says, 'No narrative . . . is so completely determinate of its meaning that it does not allow for disagreement over its interpretation.'[2] On the contrary, this feature highlighted by Wright is what gives narrative such high value in theology: the promise of narrative lies in the fact that it is not prescriptive. A story is told and people will interpret it according to their experience and insight. For instance, I recently listened to a liberal rabbi tell the story of Abraham, Isaac and Ishmael. As he told it, he knew I would hear it in ways he did not intend, and, if a Muslim imam had also been present, he would hear it differently again. But it is the same story, bearing the same meaningful truth. Together we hear the full orchestra, which is more than the melody a one-stringed violin can play or the rhythm an untuned gong can beat out. Permitted disagreements over meaning deepen, widen and strengthen the narrative.

In common with the BBC, whose purpose has always been to inform, educate and entertain, narrative has the power to inform, entertain and tell truth. Our enjoyment when listening to stories derives from natural curiosity, not only because we want to be informed of what happened next, but also because we want to learn why something happened and what the consequences were. In relation to the observation that stories entertain us – men and women have probably sat around campfires since time immemorial regaling each other with their tales of humour and terror – Wright quotes Sir Walter Scott who said that 'such is the universal charm of narrative that the worst novel ever written will find some gentle reader

2. Wright, (1988), p. 190.

content to yawn over it, rather than to open the pages of the historian, moralist or poet'.[3] I must admit that I see Scott's optimistic hopes for the worst novels as somewhat ironic. The last time I decided to read *Ivanhoe*, thinking I would relive some childhood reading as we had read it in class in my first year at grammar school, I was far from being Scott's gentle reader, and I closed the book before I suffered eye-glaze. When stories inform and entertain, we also expect them to tell truth and be true to life. We expect them to ring true to our experience and, for this reason, Wright says narrative is essentially mimetic (that is, in imitation of life), and it is a matter of faith whether the hearer or reader accepts, or believes, that the plot of the narrative gives purpose to the life it narrates.[4]

When stories inform, entertain and tell truth, they become indispensable and we would not want to be without them. We affix our self-told identities to them, we locate ourselves among our kith and kin by them, and we place ourselves in our chosen groupings – ordered on the basis of faiths, shared interests or common features – through the stories we tell of ourselves. In short, we think in narratives and use the sequences of narrative to put information associated with our lives and experiences into meaningful concepts. In the stories we tell, we explore the strangeness of the universe and discover that its mystery is ultimately knowable. Such stories become what Steven Hrotic, writing specifically about religion in science fiction, called 'life-saving mechanisms' when we apply pattern, or teleology, to the story of our lives to create autobiographies. In other words, even if, when the events were actually happening, we regarded them as random, when we retell them in retrospect we often give them a pattern and thereby attribute purpose to them.[5] Through our stories, we identify who belongs in, and who remains on the outside of, our chosen groups.

STORY IN THEOLOGY

Religion, theology and spirituality all necessarily take the form of narratives. Because narrative has been used to organise and make sense of religious experiences, and because revelation is given in narrative form, stories form the basis of religious belief and practice. George Stroup identified three styles of narrative theology. One uses story to outline the nature of a specific religion; another is religious biography; and the third style refers to biblical narratives or the Bible as a unitary

---

3. *ibid.,* p. 83.
4. *ibid.,* p. 84.
5. Hrotic, (2014) p. 188.

story beginning in Eden and ending in heaven. The first of these is
a method by which the phenomenon of religion can be studied. The
method involves identifying the story at the heart of a religion and
using that story to explain the location of religion in human experience.
This method prioritises story over experience. The second form of
narrative theology begins, on the other hand, with the experiential roots
of narrative and values the individual account of religious experience.
Whenever an individual confesses his or her faith – a practice that began
with biblical life story and became firmly established in the Christian
tradition when Augustine of Hippo wrote his *Confessions* – confession
turns into narrative. Thus, our religiosity is interpreted through the
stories we tell of ourselves. A verse I remember from childhood reminds
us that the third style of narrative theology is biblical:

> God has given us a book full of stories
> that was made for his people of old.
> It begins with the tale of a garden
> and ends with the city of gold.

Maria Matilda Penstone's children's hymn detects an overarching
canonical narrative, within which there are two other forms of story
– lesser or micro stories within the bigger narrative (including the
narrative structure of the Gospels), as well as parables, which Jesus
used as his primary teaching tool. These narratives invite interrogation,
through which the richness of the story unfolds. Wright argues that
Christian faith necessarily involves telling stories in the form of creeds
and sacraments. He suggests that the creeds follow the fourfold pattern
of the most memorable stories. These are stories that provide a setting,
theme, plot and resolution. In the case of the Nicene Creed, the opening
statement of belief in God as maker of heaven and earth sets the scene
for an outline of the theme of redemption, a summary of the plot of
Christ's life, and death and resurrection, which leads to resolution in
the last judgement bringing all human history to fulfilment.[6] Similarly,
the great prayer of thanksgiving at the Eucharist, set in the context of
thanksgiving to God as giver of all good things, carries the theme of
remembering the so-called Last Supper and has the plot of incorporating
the faithful into the kingdom of God, which is itself the final resolution
of human existence. The prayers at the sacrament of baptism also
bring the newly baptised into place within the bigger narrative, thus
ritualistically formalising the individual redemption that occurs when

---

6. Wright, *op. cit.*, pp. 88-9.

the story of God's activity in human history intersects with the personal, mundane story. At this redemptive moment, my personal story fuses with the Christian narrative, and I find my place at table.[7]

According to Wright, some of the most enthusiastic narrative theologians see telling stories as 'functionally equivalent to believing in God'.[8] Although both religious belief and storytelling involve finding meaning and order in experience, I hold back from wholeheartedly endorsing this opinion supposedly held by some narrative theology enthusiasts, simply because many storytellers are not believers. One can tell a story without believing it. Nevertheless, I agree with these narrative theologians to the extent that there is a strong correlation between telling stories and believing in God, and I affirm the image of putting your story in God's story and finding your place in God's story as a metaphor for redemption.

IMAGINATION IN THEOLOGY

Both the telling of stories and listening to them requires the exercise of imagination, which has become recognised as an important tool in the theological enterprise. David Tracy, whose publication nearly forty years ago is still frequently referred to in much contemporary theological writing, and Gordon Kaufman, whose principal thesis is that theology, by which we talk of God as the ultimate concern of human beings, is the work of human beings, have recovered imagination from the world of 'made-up-ness'. Following Tracy and Kaufman, Garrett Green has more recently named imagination as 'the anthropological point of contact for divine revelation', its *locus* or the place where revelation happens.[9]

Green began his book on imagination in theology by suggesting that the term 'imagination', which once flourished in theology only among practitioners of the academic discipline of 'religion and literature', is now receiving wider theological attention,[10] but, for a long while, imagination has been looked at with suspicion in theological circles because those who fail to distinguish between what is imagined and the imaginary think it tends towards a reductionist direction. One of Samuel Taylor Coleridge's outstanding contributions both to literary criticism and theological thought is his theory of imagination, with its implications for religion, in which he effectively 'desynonymiz[ed] Fancy and Imagination'.[11]

---

7. Stroup, (1981) p. 237.
8. Wright, *op. cit.,* p. 87.
9. Green, (1998), p. 40.
10. *ibid.,* p. 9.
11. Willey, (1949), p. 12.

Coleridge established a distinction between primary and secondary imagination in which primary imagination, which is necessarily shared by everyone, mixes together ideas or images that are already present into a mere 'mechanical juxtaposition of parts'; whereas secondary imagination, a higher and more creative faculty, fuses ideas and images in a mark of genius into the creative unity of a 'living whole or organism'. Green notes that the combined effect of this 'esemplastic power', as Coleridge called it, can be observed in one of the ways metaphor is thought to work: the primary imagination supplies the images that are then forged into creative unity by the secondary imagination.[12] So, arguing against a long tradition that regarded 'imagination' as equivalent to 'fancy', Coleridge saw imagination as 'the mind in its highest state of creative insight and awareness',[13] as the creative faculty that was the highest expression of truth.[14] For this reason, Green called us *homo imaginans*.

Later, in response to what was often heard as the rejection of religion as 'the dream of the human mind' and 'the illusory happiness of the people',[15] a distinction between realistic and illusory imagination was established that helps us to cope philosophically with problems common to both religion and literature, the problems of temporal and spatial reality when that reality is not present. Green argues that, in the case of temporal non-present reality, imagination facilitates memory of a past that is no longer present,[16] and I claim that imagination also facilitates anticipation of a future not yet present. In the case of spatial reality that is not present, imagination lets us accept the existence of a table in the next room, a Taj Mahal we have never seen before, microcosmic subatomic structures and macrocosmic astrophysics (to use Green's own examples). I suggest, too, in the same way we can imagine the settings, events and characters we read of in a novel, we can also imagine characters' beliefs. Green argued that, in theology, paradigmatic imagination through which 'we look for a pattern by which we can explore objects in a larger world'[17] assists us in our interpretation of experience and language and makes accessible something that would otherwise be beyond our linguistic grasp.[18] We can think of these sites of revelation as 'faithful imagination'.[19]

12. *ibid.*, p. 19.
13. *ibid.*, p. 16.
14. Green, *op cit.*, p. 20.
15. Feuerbach and Marx respectively, quoted in *ibid.*
16. *ibid.*, p. 64.
17. *ibid.*, pp. 69 and 78.
18. *ibid.*, p. 133.
19. *ibid.*, p. 145.

That such faithful imagination is the essence of reading is a concept whose origins may be found in the theology of Augustine of Hippo, for whom desire was the prime motivator of his religious and spiritual inclination. As Graham Ward argues, the desire to understand, which engrosses and affects readers' appetites, metabolisms, sleep patterns and physicality, circulates around the reader and the text in such a way that, in Augustine's theology of reading, reading affects both what we do and what we become. Indeed, for Augustine, reading is a spiritual exercise: 'When we read we engage with dynamics more powerful than we are aware, enter and extend the rich store-houses of our *imagination* [my italics], open ourselves to an exterior, an other which can injure as well as heal us.'[20]

It seems, furthermore, that this creative and spiritual concept of faithful imagination is related in some way to John Ruskin's concept of 'Imagination Penetrative'. Like Coleridge, Ruskin distinguished fancy from imagination and, according to Michael Wheeler, he regarded imagination as 'the highest intellectual power of man [*sic*]',[21] but, unlike Coleridge, for Ruskin imagination was more interpretative than creative. Imagination, for Ruskin, was the mind's tongue capable of piercing through whatever substantial or spiritual subject is submitted to it. Like a sea mollusc that makes holes in stones, imagination penetrates the text and allows the reader to empathise and interpret it.

Imagination enjoys this creative and interpretative role in theology as much as it does in reading. Our ability to put together the 'little pieces' of imagery to fund our imagination of the greater God has nothing to do with imaginary or illusory imagination, and everything to do with realistic imagination which we might call 'imagined reality'. For this imagined reality we may employ a rare but helpful term: irreality.[22] I am in full accord with Green when he says that, through the imagination of writers and readers, 'Fictional story . . . allow[s] us to see the world truly, as "the theatre of God's glory" in Calvin's phrase.'[23] Perhaps to image or imagine God is to believe.

THE NATURE OF BELIEF

We need to clarify what we mean by belief. One of the interlocutors in Brian Mountford's conversations, which were engendered by Philip Pullman's description of himself as a 'Christian atheist', and which

---

20. Gearon, (1999), p. 59.
21. *ibid.*, p. 8.
22. A philosophical and theological term that, unlike the more familiar 'unreality', expresses the opposite of 'reality' without denying the possibility of existence.
23. Green, *op. cit.*, p. 6.

Mountford reported in a book with that title, described three different types of belief. First, he discussed history as an evidence-based discipline in which there are competing beliefs and interpretations. Then he said that, in literature, metaphor and imagery build literary worlds where readers, through empathy, can believe in the novel's imagined world and feel what it is like to live in such worlds. This, he says, is just as much part of reality as 'prove-it science'. In the case of religion, to believe in God is to believe in the objectivity of value and purpose without evidence. In his view, religious belief is no more objective than natural intuition, personal worldview or background assumptions by which we make sense of the world around us, making belief in God possible. Note that the word he uses is 'possible', not proven. He suggests that these three types of believing do not run in parallel, independent strands, but, in reality, interlock and interweave.

In the early years of this century, an American theologian, David Cunningham, wrote an explication of the Apostles' Creed, for each clause of which he discussed either a piece of literature or a film that added insights into the doctrines enshrined in the creed. Thinking of the essentially narratival structure of the classical creeds, Cunningham finds a complementarity, rather than tension, between them and the Bible. What one says at length the other says briefly. He notes that one significant difference between the Bible and the creeds is that the creeds begin with 'I (or we) believe', while the Bible simply tells the story without needing us to state our belief in it. Moreover, we say the creeds without necessarily understanding every phrase, and without specifically acknowledging that what we are thinking when we recite them in the twenty-first century differs greatly from the way they were used in the pre-scientific age, when, for example, belief in a three-tier universe was taken for granted. Cunningham's juxtaposition of doctrinal statements with fiction highlights that there are different ways of believing, and we must establish these differences before setting about this book's task of seeing why God still finds a place in contemporary fiction in an age when religious belief no longer prevails.

The notion that there are three different ways of believing began with Augustine of Hippo who wrote of three Latin grammatical constructions describing the nature of religious belief. The first is *credere Deo*, which means 'I believe God' or I believe what God says. We use this construction in everyday discourse when we say to someone, 'I believe you', meaning that we believe that the person speaking to us is telling the truth. In the case of fiction, we might say we believe the author either because her characters and events in the novel have convinced us of the veracity of her tale, or because we accept her insights and believe the philosophical truth she seeks to communicate to her readers.

The second Latin construction is *credere Deum,* which means 'I believe God to be God.' This explicitly acknowledges that God exists and implies that the God we speak of is the only real God, but we need not do anything about that belief. Indeed, Augustine laconically added that demons and evildoers may believe God in this sense.

The third is *credere in Deum*, the clause with which the creeds begin, meaning 'I believe in God.' That little word 'in' makes all the difference. For Augustine, and for Aquinas after him, believing in God involved more than the intellect. Believing in God means that God is the object of our faith and the goal towards which our whole life is directed. According to Augustine, believing in this sense is loving God, delighting in God, walking towards God and being incorporated in God. Believing in God in this Augustinian way implies not believing in anything else; it implies exclusive devotion to God as the object or focus of our faith.

However, let us not run off with the notion that belief in God is restrictive. Belief in God can be, and should be, liberating, as Hans Küng says,

> Belief in God was and certainly often is authoritarian, tyrannical and reactionary. It can produce anxiety, immaturity, narrowmindedness, intolerance, injustice, frustration and social isolation; it can even legitimate and inspire immorality, social abuse and wars within a nation or between nations. But:
>
> Particularly in recent decades belief in God has again been able to show itself increasingly to be liberating, orientated on the future and beneficial to human beings: belief in God can spread trust in life, maturity, broad-mindedness, tolerance, solidarity, creative and social commitment; it can further spiritual renewal, social reform and world peace.[24]

As James Wood's introduction to a series of essays on literature and belief showed, the kind of religious belief that literature encourages is liberating. Wood sought to make a clear distinction between literary belief and religious belief. Fiction, he said, makes gentle requests to readers to believe. While novels require belief from the reader, the reader is not compelled to believe and can decline the implicit invitation. In contrast, Wood, Durham-born but now living in America, brought up in a Christian churchgoing family, but now expressing himself as an atheist, says that if

24. Küng, (1993), p. 14.

religion is true it must be believed in absolutely, and that once religion has revealed itself to you, you are never free because refusing to believe is categorised as denial or betrayal.[25] In the case of religious belief, belief in Something or Someone 'as if' it is true would, according to Wood, never be enough, but in reading fiction one is always free to choose not to believe. What troubles the distinction Wood makes is the special case of the New Testament Gospels. In the old estate, in pre-nineteenth-century ages, the Gospels may have been read as supernatural reports making divine truth claims, but in the 1800s they began to be read as a set of fictional tales gathered around an historical figure. At this point, the distinction between religious truth and fictional truth blurred and merged so we now live in what Wood called a 'broken estate'. Indeed, the old estate may be broken, but the new estate is an exciting and fulfilling place to live, and I hold a more optimistic view of religion than my fellow Durhamite. In my view, only bad or corrupted forms of religion restrict the individual believer, while good religion permits mature, broad-minded and variant ways of believing. Here, good religion shares common ground with literary belief, thus making reading fiction fertile ground for forming theology.

When I look back on my career so far as a theologian, I see my indebtedness both to Paul Tillich, to whom all who work in the field of religion and culture owe profound debt, and to Hans Küng, whose introduction to Christianity, *On Being a Christian*, was one of the most substantial theology books I read while preparing to study for church ministry. I want to conclude this discussion of the nature of belief by quoting a section in which Küng asks whether Christian faith is a matter of understanding, will or emotion:

> To take faith simply as an act of understanding, as theoretical knowledge, as acceptance of the truth of biblical texts or ecclesiastical dogmas, even as an assent to more or less improbable assertions: this is the intellectualist misunderstanding of faith.
>
> To understand faith simply as an act of will, as resolution of the will in face of inadequate evidence, as a blind venture, as a *Credo quia absurdum*, even merely as a duty of obedience: this is the voluntarist misunderstanding of faith.
>
> To understand faith simply as an act of feeling, as a subjective emotion, as an act of faith without any content of faith, where the fact of believing is more important then what one believes: this is the emotional misunderstanding of faith.

25. Wood, (2000), p. xv.

> Christian faith is none of these things. In absolute trust and complete reliance, the whole man [*sic*] with all the powers of his mind commits himself to the Christian message and to him whom it announces. It is simultaneously an act of knowing, willing and feeling, a trust which includes an acceptance of message and person as true.[26]

Reading, which brings the joy of immersing oneself in another's world, which stimulates new thought and provides fresh insight into old truths, and which liberates one from the yoke of bad, exclusivist, oppressive and restrictive religion is, I contend, to find a new God-given form of believing. In reading secular literature, we may encounter holiness and truth for our times.

The context for contemporary fiction

Our times form the context for this study, and we must engage with this context if we are to engage with British fiction, for, as Philip Tew, who founded the UK Network for Modern Fiction Studies, asserts, fiction cannot be segregated from its context. He argues that enjoying British fiction of our time requires us to place it within a contemporary 'larger and changing conception of Britishness'.[27] The difficulty, however, is nailing Britishness down. What *is* this Britishness? Is the changing shape of religion part of it? And, if so, what is peculiarly British about religion, faith or spirituality? This book is not a sociology of religion, but we can proceed no further without noting those aspects of the contemporary religious scene that bear on how we read of God in fiction.

The concepts of secularisation and secularity are as much the subject of academic debate as the concept of postmodernism. There is little agreement over what these terms describe, so, for the sake of this study, I will avoid using these labels. There are, however, salient factors we can identify. The first is that, over the last 100 years, Christianity has experienced a decline in the influence it once had. Most expressions of mainstream Christianity in Britain enjoyed their heyday in the years immediately before the First World War; since then, the Church has found it difficult to sustain involvement in many aspects of people's daily lives. Nevertheless, a visible presence remains. Church buildings dominate village skylines and lurk around many city street corners. The pomp and circumstance of royal, judicial and public ceremonial events usually involve ecclesiastical

---

26. Küng, (1976), p. 162.
27. Tew, (2004), p. 185.

personnel. Britain is one of the last Christian nations in the world to enshrine in its constitution a role for unelected church appointees, with bishops sitting in the House of Lords and a Speaker's Chaplain leading daily prayers in both Houses of Parliament. Even so, the Church is no longer able to influence or discipline the population's beliefs or behaviour, and, too often, it finds itself at the rear guard of reform, rushing to catch up with developments in morality when, formerly, as with pioneers such as Wilberforce and Elizabeth Fry, it might have led the way.

Second, the Church's declining influence in Britain results partly from the reduction in numbers of people engaged with organised religion. Churches remain important to many people at certain moments in their lives, but most churches have witnessed a decline in requests for the occasional offices such as baptisms, weddings and funerals. In some cases this is because churches have intentionally made themselves more inaccessible to irregular attendees by insisting on attendance at pre-baptism or pre-marriage classes. In the case of weddings, it is also because the law has been written so that ceremonies outside churches are unable to include any religious elements, and, in the case of funerals, the perception encouraged by secular officiants is that funerals led by Christian clergy are often impersonal. Because British society is a consumer society, the model is one of choice not compulsion. People may choose to use a church to mark the special moments in their lives, but many choose to go elsewhere for naming ceremonies and weddings, and choose to engage non-church officiants for their funerals.

As a result of these two factors, the British population is less educated about religion than it ever has been, despite compulsory religious education continuing to be taught in state schools. Fewer people know the Lord's Prayer. Familiarity with hymnody has reduced to the extent that many people would find it difficult to name a handful of hymns. Many in our population have never attended a Sunday service. This creates problems both for artists and for those who teach the arts. So much of our culture – its music, its art and its literature – makes no sense without its Christian context. Here lies a major difficulty for modern artists: 'Britain remains a Christian country in terms of its culture and history. Nothing will alter that. Significant sections of the population are, however, becoming not only more secular but noticeably more critical of religion.'[28] When we can no longer assume any level of religious knowledge, those who teach literature often have to establish a degree of religious understanding among their students before they can engage with the text in a meaningful way.

28. Davie, (2015), p. 37.

The third factor further complicating Britain's religious scene is that humankind's latent religiosity – for we are naturally *homo religiosus* – leads to the emergence of new rituals because people no longer feel part of institutional religion. These go unchecked by any monitoring body, and, although they may have originated in some orthodox practice, they become increasingly heterodox. Beliefs about what happens when people die offer an obvious example: illogical, but common, ideas that the deceased is a star in the sky above, or an angel looking over loved ones on earth, originate in, but veer far from, orthodox Christian notions of heaven after death. Meanwhile, latent religiosity also leads to the blurring and blending of sacred and secular, and the discovery of alternative ways to feed spiritual needs. For instance, mindfulness forms a helpful crossover between the worlds of therapy and spirituality, while, on the other hand, the gulf between church and society widens as people turn to art galleries and concert halls to find succour for their souls. As consumers, people may choose what gives them life in its fullness. Is it possible, then, that today's artists, including today's novelists, are the priests, prophets and spiritual directors of our time?

Paradoxically, the fourth factor is a turn to religion. In the latter years of the twentieth and the first decades of the twenty-first centuries, conservative and Pentecostal churches in Britain grew in number and in strength. Partly the result of migration, and partly the result of a desire both for an experiential form of worship and for clarity in doctrinal teaching, this phenomenon cannot be ignored. A cautious estimate gives a half a million as a ballpark figure for attendance in black churches of this ilk in 2015.[29] Korean, Chinese, Brazilian, Eastern European and other language-based congregations add to this number.

But the fifth factor is the most obvious and the most reported on: the perversion of religion as a weapon in both the public and personal spheres in the post-9/11 world. Abusive spirituality and expressions of faith intolerant towards people of difference, most notably in terms of sexuality, suppress individuality and impose often unwanted authority over believers. We read and hear of it most in reports from journalists reporting on the progress of violent perversions of Islam, but in each religion in the modern world violent exclusivist forms can be found. Indeed, one of the ironies of religion is that each religion carries the seeds of restoration and liberation for humanity, while also carrying the seeds of humanity's ruin. What is intended to be liberating can be constrictive. What can benefit humankind also has the capacity to cause great harm.

29. *ibid.*, p. 58.

In short, in the early years of the twenty-first century in Britain, increasing levels of secularity have been accompanied by pressing debates about religion in public life, and Grace Davie calls this a persistent paradox.

In this book, I am interested to discover where, when and how novels enter this arena of heated exchange. Why do novelists persist in writing of God? And what happens when they do? In relation to these questions, the phenomenon of church reading groups and the growth of interest in book clubs has significance, for reading groups and book clubs provide good opportunities for popular exploration of theology within literature and of the role of literature in the making of theology.

Church reading groups can provide safe places to discuss innovative ideas and alternative ways of thinking. They can deepen theological understanding and articulacy. My own experience of book clubs is that I have been a member of three. The first was The Caterpillars Literary Club, a group I joined in 1996. What was unusual about this group is that it was men-only and that, when I joined, it was in its sixty-fifth session. It had been founded as long ago as 1922, presumably by men who had not long since returned from war service. Reading groups are not a modern fad! Men from several churches met six times a year to discuss a wide range of books, including some novels, usually introduced by the member who had suggested the title. As I was a minister who showed interest in literature, one of the club members invited me to join when he was about to lead a discussion of A.S. Byatt's *Possession*. Thereafter, I chose to attend whenever a novel was being discussed. In my next church appointment, I quickly set up a reading group, called Marlborough Readers, which met monthly from January 2004 mainly to discuss novels, although an occasional biography, poetry collection or play script would break the pattern. This was a mixed-gender group made up of both retirees and people in paid employment. Up to twenty readers would gather in the host's generously proportioned lounge. At the beginning of the year we would invite nominations for books to read and agree a programme for the next six months. Not everyone who suggested a book was willing to introduce it, so we agreed who would kick the discussion into play, usually either by giving their own judgement of the book or by asking a range of questions about it. At the same time, I dabbled briefly in a book club at my local pub, having been attracted by publicity indicating that the following month they were to discuss a novel Marlborough Readers had discussed a few months previously. I was interested in finding out whether a pub discussion of Aravind Adiga's *The White Tiger* would take a course that differed in any way from that taken in a church setting. I learnt from my participation in these three groups that my interest in novels often differed from that of other participants who were more focused on characters than I was. I found my desire to explore the ideas of the novels was not always taken up by others in the groups. This may expose my interest in reading as a way of doing theology.

Silent, interiorised reading is the norm in modern times, but the popularity of reading groups reminds us that reading is essentially a social activity. It was only late in the nineteenth century that reading aloud ceased to be common. For many centuries it had been the norm, for silent reading is a more advanced skill than reading aloud. For instance, as an amateur musician I can read music, but I usually read it by playing it on the piano or singing the melody, otherwise I am limited in my ability, in my mind alone, to hear what it sounds like. So it was with the reading of texts. A frequently recounted tale tells of Augustine's astonishment when he found Ambrose, Bishop of Milan, reading silently. Even so, Ambrose was not a solitary reader; he did not read alone. He read in conversation with the author and, less directly, in consultation with editors and publishers without whom the transmission of the text would not have been possible. In the Hebrew scriptures, Nehemiah 8 records a public reading of the written law after the Jews have returned from Babylon to Jerusalem, and this event embedded the practice of public reading of the Torah in the historical life of the Jewish community. The community stands around every reading of the law. Around every act of reading stands a cloud of witnesses, conventionally referred to in literary studies as interpretive communities, a concept that goes back to a series of lectures given in 1913 by Josiah Royce.[30] His main concern in the lectures was to examine whether it remained consistent for twentieth-century Christians to hold to the ancient creeds. In the process of formulating his answer to this question, he developed the notion of interpretive communities. He argued that interpretation is a social necessity and argued for the establishment of a social order he dubbed 'a Community of Interpretation'. In the process of the interpretation of texts, the interpreter interprets a sign by producing another sign that is itself addressed to another person and calls for further interpretation. A sermon, for example, interprets a Bible passage and the sermon is in turn interpreted by those who hear it, talk about it and put it into practice. The process of interpretation is thus both temporal in that a person interprets a past into a future, and endless in that it is broken only on the death either of a particular participant in the process or of the entire interpretive group. Ideally this interpretive process links all signs and all

30. Royce, (1968).

interpreters into a single community where each component belongs, without blurring and losing their distinctive voice.[31] In other words, the vitality of a text requires ongoing conversation around it.

First-time authors quickly learn, if they did not already know, that writers do not control their texts. Writers will usually restrict themselves to one language, one style, one social register and, perhaps, one message in any single text, but a reader of that same work is unrestricted and can choose to interpret and react to an author's work in multiple ways, either intentionally or otherwise. 'No text,' said Steven Roger Fischer, 'not even the most fundamental religious, dictates to a reader.'[32] The reader controls how meaning is derived from the words the author has put on the page. If a text is regarded as ultimately, undeniably and unquestioningly authoritative, that can only be because the reader who holds that view has bestowed such authority upon it. No text can enjoy objective, immutable authority. Authors can only publish their words and set them adrift on the sea of interpretation. In this sense, the reader plays God.

Above the south door of the thirteenth-century cathedral in the northern Spanish city of Burgos, there are carvings of the apostles. They lean over to each other in seemingly animated conversation and, as they do so, they keep their places in their books with their fingers. The implication is that shared reading holds them together in community. Collective reading nurtures our spirituality and intellect. The great Quaker prison reformer, Elizabeth Fry, would have known this benefit of collective reading when, among the many reforms she campaigned for and introduced, she set up prison reading groups.

Book clubs, bolstered by Oprah Winfrey in America, Richard and Judy on British television and James Naughtie on BBC Radio 4, have increased exponentially since the late 1980s. Recent studies of book clubs in Britain have shown that many more women are attracted to them than men, that well over eighty per cent of the books being read and discussed are novels, that most book clubs prefer to read recent publications rather than classics, and that, alongside such generalist clubs, a few specialist book clubs, focusing on a particular literary genre or even individual texts such as *Finnegan's Wake*, or catering for a particular profession or workforce, can be found. Churches, which once hosted Bible reading groups in which participants shared their own response as readers to the texts, have since diversified so that general book clubs based in churches are no longer out of the ordinary. Often, however, Christian pre-understanding informs discussions of secular literature in such groups.

31. See Marshall, (1995), pp. 79-82 for a discussion of these lectures.
32. Fischer, (2003), p. 344.

I suggest six guidelines for running a successful church book club. First, the members of the group should have free choice of texts to read. It is better not to impose a choice on a reluctant group and better not to censor the selections. I remember that, when I announced that a book selected by Marlborough Readers had been changed, the assumption made by some was that I disapproved of the book. Nothing of the sort: the person who had suggested the book on the basis of reading a review only, on reading the book later, felt it was too shallow to support an evening's conversation and asked to change it. Let the group choose.

Second, I recommend adopting a regular predictable schedule, according to the appetite and time restraints of the club's members. The most common pattern is monthly meetings on a regular afternoon or evening, perhaps with a break in August, after which September's book could be a longer text, perhaps the long classic you have always wanted to read or the latest 500- or 600-page novel. I have learnt that neither occasional nor irregular book club meetings, as in my current church, rally sufficient commitment.

Third, book clubs benefit from having a designated facilitator for each session and an overseeing facilitator for the group. The latter oversees the running of the group, particularly the selection of books, the appointment of facilitators for each session and making sure the venue and hosts provide a comfortable setting. Session facilitators are responsible for starting the discussion and gently directing it, so that all who want to contribute feel neither pushed out nor derided by domineering colleagues or dominant views.

Fourth, allow discussion topics to emerge naturally when possible. *The Church Times* hosts a virtual reading group by publishing notes and questions on a book each month, having announced the choice of book in the previous month. The notes take the form of an introduction to the text, and groups could follow the questions one at a time to structure an evening's conversation. My advice, however, is not to disrupt the natural flow of conversation by moving on to what inexperienced facilitators might think of as 'the next question'. Often a free-flowing, enlightening and enjoyable conversation can begin when the facilitator simply asks, 'What did you think of it?'

Fifth, the conversation should always be open. In other words, nothing is ruled out. The dissenting voice should not silenced, and in a spirit of open-mindedness and safe experimentation, the unconventional thought should be encouraged.

As we explore God's presence in contemporary novels in this book, questions will naturally arise that could be discussed in church groups, but this is not the primary aim of *Make-Believe*. In a spirit of exploration and fun, in which the boundaries of orthodoxy are not strictly observed, we ask, 'What happens when novelists write of God?' What happens to our perception of God? Reading works best when readers foster a spirit of playfulness and fun because we learn best from play. We rejuvenate ourselves – spirit, mind and body – when we relax and have fun together. I hope that in this study of the divine in recent novels, we can relax together and feel free to ask ourselves the sometimes troubling questions novelists raise, for then our theological horizons can expand and we can draw nearer to, or deeper into, God.

* * *

The choosing of titles is a tricky business. Titles must grab attention and be an honest representation of what the book, film or artefact depicts. As I draw this introductory chapter to a conclusion, the titles of two novels and one painting come to mind. In 2002, Jon McGregor published his first novel entitled *If Nobody Speaks of Remarkable Things*. It focused on the lives of the residents of a single street in an unidentified and unremarkable English city during a single late summer's day. One of these residents is a shy, anonymous student who collects objects that have been discarded in the street, and he photographs everyday events and catalogues them in what he calls an 'archaeology of the present'. He fictionally does what the author actually does. Twenty-first-century novelists artistically record the surrounding world, lifting the mundane into a special place, re-enchanting a disenchanted world. The special spaces novels afford may be many things – magical, miraculous, spiritual, epiphanous, redemptive. They are always remarkable.

More recently, in 2017, Nick Laird published *Modern Gods*, which we will consider at greater length in the next chapter. For now, let us look no further than the title. Any book about religion in fiction is a book about remarkable things and modern gods, inasmuch as remarkable things and modern perceptions of, and images for, divinity are the raw material of contemporary fiction. They are what novels are about, sometimes explicitly and always implicitly.

In 1567, Brueghel the Elder made a picture that is usually known as *The Adoration of the Magi in a Winter Landscape* and occasionally called *The Adoration of the Kings in the Snow*. It depicts people hurrying through the streets of an imagined Bethlehem gathering fuel and heading home before a storm sets in on a freezing winter's day. We see the weather closing in. Typically, Brueghel translates the events that took place in ancient Bethlehem to a familiar sixteenth-century Flemish town so that the extraordinary is pictured within the commonplace. A secular scene plays host to the sacred. What is more, the viewer has to look carefully to see the Holy Family in the lower-left corner of the painting, hardly meriting the painting its title. I offer the strange titling of this picture as an image for what I am doing in this book. The novel is a secular phenomenon in which there are diverse genres, each hosting the sacred in the form of religious, theological and spiritual themes. Often, by focusing on these themes, I am, as it were, looking closely in one corner and this may distort the whole picture. *Make-Believe* runs this risk of distortion, but in taking the risk it sets the theological debate in its wider perspective and greater context.

Chapter 2

WRITING OF GOD AND READING RELIGIOUSLY

We turn first to literary novels. This is, of course, a misleading term because all novels are literary, but the term has come to signify high-brow, serious, arty works by academic, stylistic writers appealing to readers who look for style, innovation and serious themes in what they read. I recall a celebrity interviewee in one of those question-and-answer pages found in several Sunday magazines saying that her guilty secret is that she loves to binge-read books that she will forget as soon as she shuts down her Kindle. They used to be called 'penny dreadfuls' or pulp fiction. Literary novels are not these! Literary novels are intended to be thought-provoking and are often memorable. Writing of religion and theology in such novels is a bold move for any novelist of the twenty-first century. How can contemporary novelists be sure readers of serious fiction will be curious enough about religious practice to read about it in a novel? Even after years studying the interface between theology and literature, and after months focusing on the task of writing this book, I cannot hide how astonished I am that so many novelists still write books that are predominantly either about God or about people who believe in God.

The aim of this book is not to chart a decline in religion, but to demonstrate, through a discussion of a range of novel genres, that religion, theology and spirituality maintain their vibrancy in contemporary literature, and that, through reading fiction, religious believers can find both challenge and encouragement in their belief. As Graham Ward has said, religion once again haunts the imagination of the West.[1] Even when novels are divergent or transgressive in their theology, even when they promote an atheistic worldview or depict a dystopian world, they feed the theological imagination. They give hope for the continuing life of humanity, they give hope for a future, they give hope for God, and they give hope for a lively church in theological and ethical debate with the world around it.

1. Ward, (2003), p. vii.

In the face of contemporary novelists' continued interest in theological themes, the literary scholar Andrew Tate asks whether fiction, as a product of the disenchanted secular imagination, is capable of telling stories about God. If fiction can tell divine stories, then fiction is in a state of ambivalence: fiction is either essentially secular, telling stories of a God in whom no one can believe, or it is irresistibly religious, always assuming the existence of God. In relation to this ambivalent state, James Wood chooses to make a distinction between readers and worshippers. He argues that worshippers need unwavering faith in the object of their worship, while readers are allowed to disbelieve. Perhaps, therefore, fiction can only ever be secular? Fiction's creators know that they are dealing with true lies and that they move in the shadow of doubt, and this permits readers, at any stage, to reject what they read. Their escape route, as Tate put it, is apostasy.[2] Contrarily, Salman Rushdie's premise is that literature, even in an irreligious age, is capable of being holy or sanctified. Perhaps this happens when readers derive truth and enlightenment, glimpses of glory, whispers of grace and gasps of wonder from the novels they read. Some of the secular texts studied in this chapter rise to these heights because they open readers' eyes to what lies beyond the page. What cannot be denied is that, in the world of literature, religion has seen a revival and has been resurrected, if not as a vital element of modern life, certainly as a vital element of contemporary fiction.

The practice of religious reading underpins this book. This is the principle that critical reading of a text may include 'a faithful pursuit of textual clues until they yield a coherent religious theme, or until it becomes clear that one is lacking'.[3] The texts and their authors may give us permission to read religiously (or, if you prefer, to read Christianly), but often the permission is only implicit. Therein lies the first danger to be flagged before we discuss some specific novels – the trap of baptising all literature as anonymously Christian. Whenever we read religiously, we should be aware of the possible distortion of the text and the potential of doing violence to the author's intended meaning. We should be more sensitive about this than we have previously been, for, after all, Christians do a form of violence to the intended meaning of the Hebrew scriptures each time we read them Christologically.

This alerts us to a second danger – that of misinterpretation. In the perilous practice of reading, a text can be misinterpreted. Christians could misinterpret a Bible text as easily as a militant jihadist misreads

---

2. Tate, (2008), p. 5.
3. Haynes, (1995), p. 73.

the Qur'ān. A Christian could read the Book of Judges and believe it justifies a carpet-bombing military strategy. For reasons such as this, the critic Wayne C. Booth argued that people should not read alone. Rather, we should keep company with other readers for that will keep errant views in check. I think this is all the more important in the case of fiction because we are dealing with stories, and story is at the centre of human experience. We tell and listen to stories to make meaning of life. In older age, people become nostalgic and look back over their lives, making sense of all their experiences by narrating their lives as journey, pilgrimage, adventure, romance or confession. Stories promote the quest for wisdom and understanding. Story is the best way to do this because the weaving of story honours life's labyrinthine qualities and our mysterious perception of time. Stories can transport us to other realms from which we can clearly observe, assess and better understand our own strange world. But all that makes stories dangerous if misread or misused. So, by discussing our reading with other readers, our interpretations are brought under scrutiny and our opinions are challenged. Although Booth overstates his argument in saying we should never read alone, he has a point. We read as part of an interpretive community. Once a novel has been published and read, it is surrounded by a host of readers, each of whom is an interpreter and commentator. We join that community and become one with other readers. Darren Middleton said that, for Christians who are reading Christianly, this community is gathered at the foot of the cross, where the Christ story has a bearing on what we read.[4] As readers we are surrounded by a great cloud of witnesses.

The novels we, as an interpretive community, gather around in this chapter have all been published since 2012. They differ from each other greatly, in every respect other than that each has significant theological themes. These theological themes are the focus of my discussion of novels by Grace McCleen, Nick Laird, Neil Griffiths, Carys Bray, Tim Parks, Alex Preston and Michael Arditti.

In Grace McCleen's debut novel, *The Land of Decoration* (2012), the ten-year-old Judith has been brought up to believe in God and in an enchanted world, where miracles can be seen to happen, and where the supernatural introduces itself into everyday lives. Like her creator, McCleen, who builds a made-up world in her novel, Judith builds a model world, a land of decoration for her imagination to inhabit, which she calls 'a miracle, a paradise' made 'out of faith'. It is a better world than the real world, and is both designed and controlled by Judith. She dwells in this world she has created for herself; McCleen, too, has built

4. Middleton, (2008), p. 9.

a crazy world, where strange things happen, around which we can walk for as long as we are reading her book. Judith is a solitary child, brought up by her father who continues to mourn his wife's death in childbirth. He is a bullying puritanical presence, deeply unpopular at work because of his strike-breaking, and oppressive in the home, eventually given to irrational and erratic behaviour including building a fence to keep unwanted visitors from their home. As a member of a fundamentalist, Adventist-style church, a Christian sect known as the Brothers, he and his daughter await Armageddon by living out the Last Days with Eyes of Faith.

In the middle of her model of the Promised Land, made on her bedroom floor from bits and pieces that are transformed by her imagination (an acorn cup becomes a bowl and toothpaste tube lids become an ocean liner's funnels), Judith plays at being the Creator. There is no harm in any of her behaviour, until, after being bullied at school, she makes a wish for it to snow so that she can stay away from school. She makes it snow in her miniature world and, when the next morning there is snow outside, she becomes convinced that she has made a miracle. She hears God's voice telling her that, as God's instrument, she now possesses magical powers.

She discovers that whatever she causes to happen in her Land of Decoration also happens in the real world. She creates one miracle scene after another in her model world. To her horror they all come true. God's voice continues to urge her on, and soon all is out of control. What is going on? Her teacher worries about Judith's mental health. Her father refuses to believe Judith and dismisses it all as nonsense. As readers, we must decide for ourselves: is she mentally unstable or properly blessed with divine powers? Or is it nothing other than coincidence? The problem for the reader is that Judith's immature mind, the mind of the devout believer and the mind of God have become so interchangeable that we are never sure. Then we are told that imagination is like faith in that both see something where there is nothing. Both imagination and faith make us believe.

The Creator portrayed in this novel is, like both the novelist and her heroine, someone who is ruthlessly in control of events, one who exacts a high price for the privilege of being among the Chosen. Judith experiences God as being like the boys at school – bullying, aggressive, arrogant and sulky. Unlike other classic accounts of escapes from fundamentalism such as Jeanette Winterson's *Oranges Are Not the Only Fruit* (1985) and Edmund Gosse's *Father and Son* (1907), McCleen fictionalises the world Judith tries to leave behind. As if to prove that she has control over her narrative, McCleen obscures the era in which her story is told: Lucozade bottles wrapped in yellow cellophane place it in the same era as Winterson's childhood, but other details such as a scientist called Richard Dawkins, whom the Brothers like to argue with, suggest a more contemporaneous setting. Colin Greenland, reviewing the novel in *The Guardian*, worries that McCleen has thus destabilised her depiction of the world Judith is fleeing: if it is not real, he says, how can it harm her? If Judith lives in a made-up world, how can its religion threaten her? Both McCleen's world and Judith's model-world are fabrications, but this need not compromise McCleen's exploration of religion as a form of escapism from reality, or her discovery of an escape route for Judith from oppressive religion into freedom.

Judith's Land of Decoration, her father's repressive absolutist faith and McCleen's alternative are worlds that function as inhabitable myths. These interest the central character in Nick Laird's third novel, *Modern Gods* (2017). She is Liz, an anthropologist who has written a successful self-help book entitled *The Use of Myth: How Levi-Strauss Can Help Us All Live a Little Better*. The novel crosses between two religious cultures: that of Northern Ireland and that of the fictitious island of New Ulster off the Papua New Guinea coast where the world's 'newest religion' is developing. Laird has said in interview that the book alternates between 'realities'. These fictitious realities help him explore the nature of belief.

Modern Gods begins with an atrocity: two men in comedy Halloween masks walk into a pub, shout, 'Trick or treat?' and shoot seven people dead. This is the appalling outcome of the worst form of religion. In Londonderry, religion, as expressed in the defaced roadside signs and the wayside pulpit notices outside gospel halls, feels sinister and threatening. Will the world's newest religion in Papua New Guinea fare any better?

In New Ulster, Liz and her team, whose aim is to film a television documentary, seek out the emerging religious movement and meet the prophet Belef, whose followers fetishise Western items and images that were abandoned on the island during the years of colonialism. Belef has lapsed from the Christianity Westerners had brought to the island and developed a new religion called The Story. Followers of The Story await divine liberation when the new Jesus will come and give them what is rightfully theirs – autonomy in New Ulster. Liz's initial analysis is that The Story is a four-fold syncretic blend of some local religions with Christianity mixed with imagery of Western technology, such as aeroplanes and tractors, which appeared magical to indigenous people, and a 'bit of political independence' thrown in.

Meanwhile in Ulster, Liz's family is struggling as her mother, Judith, tries to hide the fact that her cancer has returned and her sister, Alison, comes to terms with the discovery that her new second husband was one of the shooters involved in the Halloween pub massacre. Judith's visit to a faith healer epitomises the inefficacy of her native religion: the healer takes a prayer card from a bookshelf stuffed with John Grisham and Patricia Cornwell novels and instructs her to lean on an eighteen-inch-tall bogwood cross while her husband Ken repeats the prayer three times. In payment for this therapy, they donate the suggested fifty euros, and, as they drive away, Judith feels the warmth of the prayer and blessing fade.

In her final assessment of The Story, Liz acknowledges that although she has spent her life 'studying the differences, how one tribe does this, another that', there is in fact little difference, 'just tiny variations on a theme of great suffering, great loss' (299). That there are more parallels than there are distinctions means that Laird, in setting New Ulster's new religion alongside Ulster's damaging Protestantism, offers a darkly comic satire of religion's inevitable inadequacy and its necessity. Liz writes, 'in fact any story . . . acts as an excursion into the hyper real. The dailiness we inhabit is replaced by a copy of the world, one where we find closure . . . it is a story, a litany of anecdotes and mythologies. . . . It's a plural vision' (252). While the title of this novel raises the question, 'Who are the gods of the modern age?', what Modern Gods is about is the necessity of stories of gods – any gods or any God – what the critic Elizabeth Lowry, writing her review in The Guardian, called 'the human need to believe in something, and of the stories, religious and secular, we live by'. Often we choose to live by them despite their contingency, their inadequacy and their finiteness. Indeed, the power of story lies behind all literature, as much as it lies behind religion. This is why both are significant to people because we lead storied lives.

In both Ulster and New Ulster, Modern Gods presents damaging pictures of religion, and I cannot be certain whether Laird gives any hints of better forms of religion. What Laird presents seems utterly broken.

The title of Neil Griffiths's novel As a God Might Be (2017), words taken from Wallace Stevens's poem 'Sunday Morning', suggests a more monotheistic focus than Modern Gods. As a God Might Be found its publisher when, at a small-press fair, the novelist commented that he was writing a theological novel. I imagine this was far from being an easy sell in an age of religious illiteracy! The novel discusses more than theology, but it is the subject of some lengthy discourses within the book.

Reminiscent of the legend of St Cuthman, who built a church where he dropped a wheelbarrow in which he carried his crippled mother, and of Golding's novel *The Spire*, which tells of a dean erecting a spire on his medieval cathedral against expert advice, this novel tells of Procter MacCullough's building of a home and a church on the edge of a cliff, where planning permission is not required for religious buildings. His approach is similar to that of those who built the Temple in the Old Testament both in its precision and its use of cedar and larch. At least twice, the local vicar asks if he is building an Ark using cubits as a unit of length (43 and 150). If the original plan had been for an orthodox design, the end result is weird – 'not a church church' – and the steeple, which is only 'a kind of steeple' stands as both an expression of yearning and a depiction of fallenness. The building represents both human aspiration and failure.

MacCullough (Mac) gathers three local young men and a young woman, Rebecca, to serve as a permanent team of assistants. Back home his wife, Holly, and their children, Walter and Pearl, see his enterprise as a mid-life crisis (90-1). Indeed, his dalliance with Rebecca and her mother, Judith, suggests there is an element of truth in this perception, especially as Mac does not describe himself as a Christian believer in any normative sense.

Mac's perception is that Britain is a post-religious country (31), to all intents and purposes a secular state where cultural Christianity prevails. He is reluctant to state any belief in God (34) largely because he finds the question 'Do you believe in God?' meaningless. When he is pushed to define God, Mac says, 'God is the transcendent Other for whom creation . . . is a gratuitous act of love. . . . A gift from his infinite excess. . . . That we can know him at all is because of the possibility of this excess within us, which we experience as love, art, great feats of the mind' (86).

Conscious reference to Dostoevsky and to Rowan Williams's work on that great Russian writer recurs throughout the book, as if Griffiths intends the novel to be seen as a *The Brothers Karamazov* for the present age. Mac is not without his fair share of family suffering – his father-in-law Edward has MS and his son is on the autistic spectrum.

Mac's 'mission' had begun with a vision of sorts. Intense feelings about a sense of purpose in his life cause him concern because he is sure that the predominantly physical embodiment of this is not mystical, but simply that the world felt full and explicit in its 'thereness' (92). Something similar had happened to him previously, and he ruminates on where he could get help to deal with such a matter – from a vicar, a therapist (whether a believer or not) or a neurologist (96-7). Indeed, he asks, is sensing God a disorder that requires therapy (95)? What does the modern scientific world say of this? Where lies the boundary between mental illness and religious experience?

Transcendence is easy – young ravers feel it on Ibiza every weekend – while Otherness, by which I mean being confronted with a sense of something and only being able to define it as Other, is more difficult to express (195). One of Mac's group, Simon, observes that Milton succeeded in creating places that did not exist, yet were somehow nevertheless recognisable. He suggests this defines Otherness. This creation of Otherness as a recognisable non-place is the novelist's role: it is what Griffiths does.

About midway through the novel, Mac experiences a moment of uncertainty (331). After a crisis at work, he looks over the building site. Feeling distracted and lost, he wonders whether it is all 'imagination' or 'the moment God passed by' (331). He tells Rebecca the nature of his mystical experience – a miraculous fall from the cliff (400-7) – in which he realises the uncreatedness and self-sustenance of God (403). Yet he says we are like God in that we too have freedom to use love and power.

Tragedy intervenes when in a dispute between Mac's followers, Terry decapitates Nat. Later, there are tender scenes between Mac and Terry's bedridden mother, after which Mac determines to help Terry. Mac had no idea whether Terry had found God when, before the murder, he had withdrawn into himself and, using the Bible, had escaped into another world that was as complex as his own, but richer with possible meanings. Mac wonders if Terry were subjected to psychiatric examination, would he be declared insane? Is his killing of Nat any more or less a symptom of psychosis than Mac's claim that he had encountered God (426)?

In conversation with Judith, Mac, who has just been thinking of Pascal's Wager and his feeling that he is justified in placing his bets on God (442), contrasts sacred with secular saying the former is 'out of time' and the second is 'in time' (443). Harking back to Salman Rushdie's claim that all literature can be sacred, Griffiths may here have hit on *how* and *why* secular literature can be sanctified into sacred texts capable of speaking of holiness and God. Are secular texts lifted into becoming sacred because they are 'out of time', dealing with matters of eternity, transcendence and imagination?

Intertextuality, whereby dialogue between texts occurs, can be unintentional and accidental because it is often subjective. When, for instance, I read that Mac feels that most people will encounter his church as merely a relic of a particular summer, though a nice place to be as a place of reflection and solitude (485), I remembered Philip Larkin's accidental visit to a church in his poem 'Church Going', in which he muses on what will happen to churches when no one goes there anymore. Will they be 'not worth stopping for', or will people still call in because they recognise that these are serious places on serious earth? However, there are no intentional hooks or clues in the novel's text to prompt other readers to note the same intertextuality.

When, later in the novel, Rebecca and Mac take Terry for palliative care, after his release from prison for compassionate reasons, Griffiths reflects on the nature of humankind (506). Mac concludes,

> There was nothing unalterable about human beings. Killing someone, killing Nathaniel didn't make [Terry] irredeemable and damned. There was no equation of behaviour, no divine judgment, that condemns people to that outcome, whether they want it or not. People commit worse crimes, and live full happy lives. You can do a lot of terrible things, and still go on living well – we are strong that way. Committing terrible acts is as compatible with living a happy life as devoting yourself to ministrations of mercy, pity and love (522).

We can choose what we do and how we live, and we live on. Terry's murderous actions may have been a test. In killing Nat, Terry was possibly trying to force the hidden or absent God into the open. Or, Griffiths suggests, citing the near-sacrifice of Isaac by his father, Abraham, it may have been a cry into the silence (523). Later, as Mac sits by Terry's deathbed wondering, first, what Terry's experience of God had been and, second, what his experience of death was like, Mac acknowledges that, for some, God is 'the presence of absence' (563).

Griffiths's author's note to his novel draws attention to the chapter entitled 'Apocrypha' as being potentially offensive to Christian believers, in that he sees it as a challenge to the Christian Communion. The chapter takes the form of Mac's monologue addressed to the dying Terry. It compares both Buddhism and Islam with Christianity, it discusses the doctrine of Original Sin and gives Mac the opportunity to describe himself as a 'tragic Christian' in acknowledgement of human hopelessness (544). Thus, to the two deaths in this novel – Nat's violent death for which no one was prepared and Terry's lingering death – a third is added, this time to do with Mac, but what kind of death is this? Does Mac die to his 'family of love' (which had been the working title of the novel)? Or does his vision die?

The novel ends with a sermon on the beach as Terry's body burns on a homemade funeral pyre. In my previous book, *The Novel as Church: Preaching to Readers in Contemporary Fiction*, I suggested that when a sermon is placed at the end of a novel, this enhances the sermon's significance as an authoritative text and the sermon becomes more important as a tool for interpreting the novel. In the case of the fictional sermon I was discussing at the time – in Michael Arditti's *Easter* – it formed a 'useful summation of the novel's implied theology'.[5] This is so with this funeral sermon, which begins by facing the fact that Terry committed the most terrible act and refers to Terry's torment: he had felt that there was no freedom in just being good, he believed that only those who offend others or offend God are authentic (592). Mac argues that we must look for what is Good (594) and that living a good life is placing love at its heart (594). 'We must love Terry. Killer of our friend. Killer of our son.' He gives no instruction and utters no commandment in the sermon, but invites hearers to choose between believing in God, who puzzles us by allowing atrocities to happen, and coming to the conclusion that there is no God (596). God's gift to us, he says, is the freedom to love. His sermon ends as his voice is choked with smoke from the funeral pyre, but he has nothing left to say. He had said nothing, but neither had he remained silent (597), although his daughter, Pearl, remarks, 'It was nice what you said, Daddy.' The preacher and the pastor in me lead me to wonder whether this is the essential nature of theology. Comforting the bereaved, caring for the dying and being alongside the hopeless affect the capacity to preach assuredly and reassuringly Sunday by Sunday. Theology may be rendered speechless, and silence becomes more powerful than words.

Novelists who choose to write of God, as well as those who write of characters who believe in God, must feel some of this compulsion to speak about that for which no words are adequate. I suspect that sometimes it is their exasperation with believers who are adamant in their mistaken beliefs that drives them on in their quest. One such writer is Carys Bray whose debut novel, *A Song for Issy Bradley* (2014), is set in a Mormon household. Bray was herself brought up in a Mormon family, but left the church in her early thirties thereby, according to the novel's dustjacket, replacing religion with writing. Her art implies that she holds residual faith. Set in an intensely religious household where the head of the family, Ian Bradley, is a Mormon bishop who shows little loving care to his family and who teaches the children in the congregation to be both sacrificial and obedient, the novel shows

5. Dickinson, (2013), p. 41.

how the family responds to the sudden death of the eponymous Issy after she contracts meningitis. As Issy lay ill, Ian strode into her sick room and commanded the illness to leave, pinning the failure of his command on the lack of faith displayed by Issy's mother, Claire. He refuses to mourn as those without hope would mourn and believes that Issy is blessed because, as one who died under the age of eight years, she will go straight to heaven. Claire, on the other hand, who wants to grieve honestly, is denied all opportunity for grief. Ian expects her simply to pick herself up, dust herself down and start over again. When she retreats to Issy's bunkbed and lies there, having failed to collect her son Jacob from school, take drying clothes in from the line or wash the dirty dishes, Ian has no idea how to respond to her bereavement. Issy's siblings are left to flounder, too. Zippy, dissecting a frog in a biology lesson at school, wrestles with the nature of personhood: 'people are more than their bodies. Zippy isn't sure about the mechanics of it, but when Issy climbed out of herself. She didn't leave anything behind, she took all the bits that made *her* – what's left is empty' (121). The clichéd condolence cards the family receives from church members reveal a contorted theodicy, which suggests that those who suffer are especially blessed, and that the growth that comes through suffering is such that suffering should be sought and welcomed. This is sufficiently disturbing to give Christian readers cause to examine the words of condolence and sympathy cards they use: does their piety hinder their intention? Is silence in the face of tragedy often better?

Sexual relationships and marriage are as poorly dealt with in the Bradleys' Mormon Temple as bereavement is. Temple elders manipulate girls into dreaming of a perfect marriage, to dress up in their mother's wedding dresses and get their mothers to write about their own marriages, with the expectation that this will encourage them to emulate their mothers' examples. Zippy, of course, must herself write her mother's supposed letter to the elders because Claire is in no fit state to dissemble and write how wonderful her marriage to Ian has been. In the Temple, girls are given leaflets about 'dating decisions' to keep them virtuous and are instructed to fill in a 'Young Women's Wedding Guide', in which they idealistically describe their perfect match and plan their weddings. Zippy does not need to imagine her future husband, for she is already in a relationship with Adam and, when they are discovered in a passionate clinch, Zippy is interrogated by the Temple President. He tells her boys are only after one thing and that she should ask for God's forgiveness. She excuses Adam by accepting the president's explanation that girls make it hard for boys and that, by wearing a pretty dress, she was 'walking pornography'. The narrator comments, 'What happened between them was lovely but it was *wrong*' (284).

Adults in the Temple hold a variety of beliefs that Bray gently holds up to readers both for ridicule and to be contested. These include keeping handcarts on standby so they can escape back to Utah as soon as signs of the end of the world at the second coming of Christ are evident, as well as Bishop Rimmer telling of Jesus visiting America sometime after he was crucified. Bray implicitly asks readers to assess the irrationality of such beliefs held by supposedly mature believers by placing them alongside children's behaviour. Jacob, for instance, prays over a dying goldfish to effect resurrection in imitation of his father's prayers over the sick and dying. Later, there is a telling exchange of views between Sister Anderson and Issy's other brother, Alma. Jacob has boasted at Sunday school of resurrecting the dead goldfish and Sister Anderson, supposedly out of concern for Jacob, tells Alma. Sister Anderson has herself made similar resurrectionist claims, namely that, when she was at the Temple, she saw Issy alive though she was long since dead. Alma challenges her: 'I am sure you weren't telling lies . . . but you need to learn the difference between make-believe and real life' (302). The beliefs held by the adults in this novel are at times irrational and its children challenge them. Out of the mouths of babes . . .

That this novel is primarily about faith is evident when Claire, who Bray describes as 'so very lost', walks along a beach in the final section entitled 'Footprints in the Sand'. The novel having opened with Claire dreaming of walking along a beach with Jesus who declares his love for her, this epilogue now reminds many readers of a short sentimental piece often read at funerals, where a believer accuses God of desertion and betrayal because, on looking back, there is only one set of footprints in the sand. The explanation is that God was carrying the believer. In *A Song for Issy Bradley*, however, Claire dare not look back because she does not want to suffer Lot's wife's fate, but the reader knows there is only one set of prints in the sand. The beach's shoreline marks for Claire the border between heaven and earth, and she wavers between faith and doubt that God will come. The flatness of the beach and sea mean that she could almost believe that the earth is flat, and that if she swam out far enough she would simply drop off the edge into heaven (394). As she looks to the horizon, she sees 'there is nothing but the spare spread of the sea and bare heaven' (396). Bray keeps Claire's 'lonely, waterlogged footprints' open to the reader's own interpretation: are they evidence of a person abandoned by God or of one who, despite the oppression of her church's odd beliefs and practices, has found a sense of peace in the God who is beyond human religious practices.

The remarkable achievement of *A Song for Issy Bradley* is that it is faith-affirming while making a strong critique of oppressive and abusive religion, which damages the Bradley family and others in so many ways. The ill-effects of religion in the novel include the unbending expectation of obedience and sacrifice, the denial of any opportunity to grieve naturally, the false hope of healings and revivification, unanswered prayers, enforced morality, misogyny, and total intolerance of outsiders and non-believers. The novel encourages readers to ask whether the belief that everything happens to people for benign reasons is any more rational a belief than children's beliefs in tooth fairies, Father Christmas or Easter bunnies. Over against such bad religion, the novel portrays the positive effects of religious faith. It portrays people who live on a metaphorical shoreline, always on the border between life and death, heaven and earth, always on the margins. The footprints we leave behind show that we walk alone, and among the characters in the novel Alma at least learns to stand up for himself against bullies in the Temple. When Ian and the surviving children call Claire home, she responds positively and returns – an important indication that there is something of value in the Mormon household that Claire does not want to lose. What is hopeful about this novel is that it shows people's power to overcome tragedy without resorting to clichéd piety or restrictive religion.

Some novelists are born into circumstances that give them profound insights into the religious mind. Both Tim Parks and Alex Preston are sons of clergymen, and many of Tim Parks's novels, including his 2016 novel, *Thomas and Mary*, have explored the difficulties associated with being a clergyman's son. Its subtitle describes the book as a love story and it anatomises a somewhat taken-for-granted thirty-year marriage as it collapses because of Thomas's infidelity. Shortly before writing this novel, Parks published *Where I'm Reading From* in which he argued, on the basis of his reading of Dickens, Joyce, Hardy and Lawrence, that the style and the content of a novelist's work are inevitably coloured by personal experience, and that the writing of novels can be a survival strategy by which the novelist comes to terms with tensions within and around his or her own family. Sometimes I feel sorry for novelists' families! However, unusually for contemporary fiction, Parks felt he needed to have a disclaimer at the beginning of *Thomas and Mary* insisting that it is a work of fiction, that Thomas and Mary have never existed and that any similarity to real persons is entirely accidental. Not everyone is inclined to believe the disclaimer for it remains tempting to see Tim Parks himself in his character Thomas Paige. Like Parks, Thomas is the son of a clergyman.

The fact that one of the novel's chapters, 'Reverend', had previously been published as a short story in *The New Yorker* betrays the episodic nature of the novel, which is almost a collection of linked short stories. It ranges back and forth both in time and in voice, from chapter to chapter, with each chapter capable of standing alone as a short story. In each chapter, a different facet of Thomas and Mary's failing relationship is examined. The relationship has become stale over the years as petty resentments have eroded any love there was between them. Now the novel follows the twists and turns of its breakup. The louder voice in the book is Thomas's, but when we hear Mary's it is insistent. At one point she complains to Thomas that he does not love the Lord Jesus. 'I keep thinking that,' she says, 'and it grieves me. More than anything else in the world' (118). Because this is her greatest complaint against her husband, religion plays a bigger part in this novel than one might otherwise have expected. Three aspects of religion in the novel merit attention.

First, Mary is depicted as an evangelical Christian. When Thomas insists in a mealtime philosophical discussion that mind and body are inseparable, she resists the idea. As one who had had a double mastectomy some years previously, her own view is that, as her body aged and declined, she felt increasingly separate from it, and she was most emphatically '*not* her cancer' (125, original italics). She persists in the belief that, after her eventual death, she would enjoy eternal life in heaven while her body will remain in the earth until Resurrection Day. Thomas finds such conservative expressions of religion abhorrent, yet is later relieved that she does not lose this faith when she is dying in a hospice bed. She is, and always will be, Mrs P (127).

Second, faith is seen in the novel as identity-giving in that Mary's religious faith is part of who she is. The same is true of Thomas. The chapter 'Reverend' describes the relationship Thomas had had with his father. The strength of Thomas's father's religious beliefs, not only recorded in his unpublished book on the Holy Trinity, but also witnessed in a six-month period when a wave of enthusiasm flowed through his father's church, reinforces Thomas's sense of inadequacy and religious scepticism (248). Echoing the letter to the Laodiceans in the Book of Revelation, Thomas dubs himself 'Mr Lukewarm' (244). The chapter ends with an image of Thomas as a boy swimming in the sea while on holiday at Deal while his father anxiously watches and calls him back lest he swim too far out. In life, has Thomas swum so far away from his father that there is no way back (253)? Perhaps the reason he has swum away from his religious roots is that they have suppressed his true self. Only a short while before that holiday, his father had weaponised his religion as he tried to exorcise 'demons' from Thomas's brother to enforce good behaviour.

Third, theology and faith are depicted as earthly concerns. In a chapter entitled 'Martha and Edward', a conversation between Thomas's parents after their deaths is imagined. It amusingly depicts heaven as a place where there are no Bibles, no doctrine and no discussion of theology because 'it just doesn't seem to matter any more' (309). It is plain that Thomas and Mary's marriage is stifling because their shared religion stifles and traps them, even though, in its purer form (as seen in Parks's light-hearted depiction of heaven), religion liberates. This might lead us to ask of ourselves, 'How does my faith define me?'

Turning now to Alex Preston, whose second novel, *The Revelations*, published in 2012, was described by one reviewer as admirably bold because Christian believers may struggle with its hypocritical characters, while non-believers are likely to be impatient with the novel's intricate descriptions of what happens in the Course that four university friends join in order to find meaning for their lives. The Course is led by a charismatic priest called David Nightingale and is a thinly veiled fictionalisation of the real-life Alpha Course run in many churches throughout Britain. The four friends are a married couple, Abby and Marcus, and an unmarried couple, Lee and Mouse. Each of these is a confused soul – Marcus is a melancholic borderline alcoholic who is far from confident in his Christian faith, Abby struggles to cope with the aftermath of several miscarriages, Lee has been described as 'the girl every man wants to sleep with' and she tends to reciprocate, while Mouse tags along as a friend with whom she will not sleep. All four have made the wrong romantic choices and have become involved with the Course largely to avoid having to face up to mistakes. The Course serves as a crutch to lean on while its participants work out who they are. Although Abby, Marcus, Lee and Mouse are supposed to be the 'moral leaders' in this world, it takes Rebecca – a young woman who has a drunken fumble with Marcus at a party – to voice what the readers are very soon thinking. 'Seriously, you need to get out of the Course,' she tells him. 'Those aren't good people you have been telling me about. You're better than that' (257).

David Nightingale's ambition is to spread his Course across the globe, which depends on the success of the four group leaders in attracting a large number of new recruits. David admits that the Course was designed as the Church's response to its crisis with young people and its failure to engage with them. His assessment was not that the younger generation was a 'Godless generation', but that the Church no longer spoke young people's language (318). One who attended the group that Lee ran expected that the Course would be a way of 'making myself believe, of convincing myself that it all means something' (41), but he expresses his intention not to return for the next session, as he feels it will not do him any good. Like the real-life Alpha Course and other similar programmes, the Course is an attempt at evangelistic make-believe: it intends to convince attendees and convert them to the Christian faith.

The book touches on several contemporary religious hot potatoes. The first is that of creating religious personae. When Lee expresses dark thoughts, Mouse accuses her of self-pity and constant misery and says she must pull herself together. The problem, he says, is that she has forged an identity for herself around religion: 'Lee the sexy little party girl has been replaced by Lee the pious saint. But it's not a good religion, not a real one' (115). Often when a person comes to faith he or she is encouraged to leave the old self behind, but I, as a minister in a church where some congregants previously belonged to other faiths, want to ask how such people can be their true selves in their discipleship if they have left behind the formative experiences of their childhood homes, other cultures and other worshipping communities. How can they honour their traditions and bring their old selves to their new faith? How can they maintain the integrity of their identity? And what are the dangers of creating new religious identities for ourselves?

Second, the novel discusses sexual ethics. In a sermon given to new recruits on the Course in the early chapters of the novel, David claims that, although some will find that the Course is not for them, it is not an exclusive club. Rather, all who will respect and abide by its rules, are welcome. Nevertheless, he sets down some quite restrictive guidelines when he addresses the allegation that the Course is outmoded and old fashioned, admitting that the allegation carries some truth and outlining a traditionalist view of marriage, which promotes celibacy before marriage and the belief that marriage between a man and a woman has the love that 'is recognised in the eyes of God' (62). David is also fiercely and offensively critical of Lee's sexual promiscuity – 'you have become known as a slut' (68). Philip challenges David's views because he thinks his conservatism and accompanying homophobia will deter many young people who struggle with sexuality (64). Readers will find themselves torn between being 'with' Philip or David, and some, such as me, will feel heartbroken that there seems to be no place within the Course family for gay men or women.

Third, I note that David manipulates Bible texts for his own ends. For instance, one of the Course followers discusses Jesus's saying about the rich man, the camel and the eye of the needle (admittedly, a text about which many discomforted people have offered tortuous readings). David follows it with a comment about the Course not judging people on the way they behave in office because 'it would be ridiculous to expect people to behave like saints in a world that is as dog-eat-dog as ours' (140). Scandal hits the Course family when Lee is found dead and her body is moved. David wants, above all else, to suppress the scandal and avoid publicity. He would have to resign with the consequence that all the 'good' the Course had achieved would be undone (284).

Fourth, Lee has a special interest in female mystics, notably Hildegard, Catherine of Siena and Margery Kempe, and this highlights the novel's interest in the role of women in religion. Mouse alleges that these women are hysterics who cannot help Lee. They are, Lee retorts, her role models, and Julian of Norwich, of whom she is particularly fond, was no hysteric. She very quickly shows that weeping hysterics are not her only model of religious womanhood. When a drunken banker slaps her bottom, she runs after him and stabs him in the neck with a pencil, thinking all the while of Judith slaying Holofernes who had to act heroically because none of the men around her would assist (118). It is troubling for modern-day Christianity that both the Christian Bible and Christian history are mostly patriarchal in their worldview and depict women as 'maidens or harlots', sexualised, vilified and marginalised. The novel's allusions to female mystics introduce an alternative image or model of womanhood to a community following the Course that, by and large, otherwise endorses patriarchy.

Finally, at one point in *The Revelations*, Lee alludes to Venerable Bede's sparrow, a parable in which Bede compared our lives to the flight of a sparrow from the cold dark of night into the warm light of a bright mead hall. Lee says, 'We fly from darkness into light and laughter and then out again into darkness' (114). The image depresses her. This image is well known, well worn and often used. It usually conveys something of the transience of life. Interestingly, it does not include any sense of moving from this life into a better existence, for the bird flies back out into the cold night! I like to use it as an image for the reading experience in that readers fly in and out of the fictional (hopefully vivid) world of a novel.

The novel ends with an allusion to Julian of Norwich. Mouse reads a passage from Julian's *Showings* (the now-preferred English title for the book previously known by the more Latinate title shared with this novel, *The Revelations,* or, more fully, *The Sixteen Revelations of Divine Love*). In the passage Mouse reads, Julian writes of miracles coming after sorrow. The novel's last words quote Julian's well-known prayer: 'All shall be well, and all shall be well, and all manner of thing shall be well.' After the novel has depicted such a manipulative form of Christianity, such that the novel could be read as a satire of common forms of Christianity in Britain today, I find it difficult to be sure whether Preston's concluding sentences express his own optimism for the faith in which he was nurtured in his childhood home, or whether they form a further critique of the blind faith of gullible believers.

Finally, in this chapter, we turn to Michael Arditti whom the critic Peter Stanford suggests has inherited the mantles of noteworthy theological writers such as Muriel Spark, Graham Greene and Evelyn Waugh,[6] and whom Philip Pullman has called 'our best chronicler of the rewards and pitfalls of present-day faith'.[7] *Of Men and Angels* (2018) seeks to reclaim the biblical story of Sodom and Gomorrah, which Arditti identifies as 'the cornerstone of gay oppression' because most people read it as a strong denunciation of homosexuality, although the Old Testament prophet Ezekiel saw it as a myth about pride and Christ saw it as a story of inhospitality. Arditti tells stories from five eras, each story challenging the conventional reading of the original Sodom and Gomorrah story. The novel almost falls into five distinct novellas, but they are held together, first, by the overarching role of Gabriel who travels through the ages and introduces each section and, second, by the fact that, during each era, the authority of scripture was being challenged in some way. Arditti sets each section in a period in which the science of hermeneutics reached a new stage in its evolution. During the Babylonian exile, in which the first section is set, the Hebrew scriptures were formed. Among the scribes in the novel who fret about the reception of the text from various irreconcilable sources, which forces them into interpretative compromise and restyling of the texts (including the Sodom and Gomorrah narrative) is Jared, a pious boy educated in the court of King Nebuchadnezzar. When his homosexual experiences lead him to challenge the orthodox interpretation of the Sodom story, he is taken off the project and the more conservative interpretation of the Sodom narrative prevails.

The Middle Ages provide the context for the novel's second section that tells of the guilds preparing mystery plays for performance on the streets of York. The Guild of Salters is responsible for the scene that tells

6. In a review of *Of Men and Angels* in *The Observer* on 25 March 2018.
7. Interviewed by Sarah Meyrick in *The Church Times* on 23 March 2018.

the story of Lot and his wife. Dramatic interpretation of the texts causes concern and debate about what taking religious stories out of churches onto the streets does to the texts. Some opposed such street dramas because they felt that taking the story out of churches compromised its sacredness. A similar debate took place many years later, in the middle of the twentieth century when Dorothy Sayers wrote a radio play telling the Jesus story. Even then, some felt it was inappropriate for an actor to play Jesus! We will return to this issue in a later chapter when we consider modern novels retelling biblical stories. Does retelling or relocating the narratives reduce their power as authoritative texts?

Arditti sets the third section in Renaissance Florence and portrays the struggles that the artist Sandro Botticelli had when trying to depict Sodom in a manner that would be considered acceptable in Savonarola's reactionary city. Again, the conservatives sought to restrain liberal interpretation and development.

The middle years of the nineteenth century, when the development of biblical criticism upset the certainties of some believers, are the setting for the fourth section. When interviewed, Arditti called this 'a great age of doubt'. Here he tells of a 'biblical archaeologist', a priest and amateur archaeologist who sets out to establish the historicity of biblical narratives. In this instance, he searches for the ruins of Sodom.

The final section is based in 1980s Hollywood, where a closeted gay actor, dying of AIDS, makes one last film and stars in a controversial reimagining of Sodom. This was an era when AIDS was seen by some as a second Sodom and God's punishment.

As you may deduce from those brief introductions to each section, there is a lot of sex in this book and very little of it is behind closed bedroom doors, but the primary foci of the novel are religious hypocrisy and the formation and reception of authoritative texts and narratives. At one point in the third section, Savonarola preaches a vituperative sermon in which he lists all the offences the city of Florence must confess so that its people can 'escape the wrath of the Avenging Angel' (223), and he reserves his strongest venom for a diatribe against homosexuality. He adjures his hearers to spit on any 'sodomite . . . so as to douse the flames of his lust' (224). After more than an hour of preaching, Savonarola tells of a dream in which he was presented to the Virgin Mary who told him that 'if Florence wishes to regain God's favour, [the city] must build a pyre in the piazza and pitch every sodomite into the flame' (225). Before saying this, however, she had cupped her hands around the ears of the baby she was cradling. Savonarola thought this was to protect Christ's ears from hearing how awful the sins were. I suspect that Arditti adds this detail to the dream's account, not to protect Christ from sin, but to show that Christ will not be party to the Church's persecutions and homophobia.

The pattern repeated in the first four sections of Arditti's novel, whereby the conservative traditionalist reading of the Sodom narrative prevails and the homophobes seem to win, does not engender hope. However, the final section breaks this mould and ends with a beautiful vision that draws on the novel's archangelic prologue: Frank Archer, the Hollywood actor, dies hallucinating that he is meeting Archangel Gabriel, and the moment of his death coincides with a voice shouting 'Action!' and Frank taking a leap of faith. Contrary to the centuries of persecution of gay men and women by heterosexuals, Frank receives divine affirmation and is accepted into God's presence. If this does not give the world hope for the establishment of a lively church in open acceptance of all humanity, little will.

Many of the novels discussed in this chapter embed the Christian Bible in their text in some way. In some cases, characters bandy around Bible verses as proof that the text supports their behaviour or beliefs, and, in the case of Arditti's novel, the interpretation of one of the Bible's stories over the centuries of its transmission forms the basis of the book. The overall effect of the juxtaposition of Bible and novel is that the status of the Bible as an authoritative text is brought into question for Christian readers.

One of the prevailing characteristics of the twenty-first century is people's suspicion of authority. Discussion of religious authority and authoritative texts was destabilised when, on 11 September 2001, religious fundamentalists, bolstered by perverse readings of the Qur'ān, aimed their peopled weapons at buildings symbolic of Western culture with devastatingly fatal effect. Some of these terrorists recited, and others carried, proof texts from the Qur'ān. Now 9/11 marks the beginning of an era where religions are viewed as absolutist claims on truth, in contrast with the surrounding culture that is always in a state of flux, and this jeopardises any relationship religion has with culture. The post-9/11 era is far less stable than the years before. Any tendency towards fundamentalism in religion makes discussion of authority in religion and its texts difficult, but, paradoxically, even more essential if the problem of religion is to be addressed in the twenty-first century. The novels discussed in this chapter, in a small way, have demonstrated that literature is capable of offering a lifeline to rescue the present age from the clash of truth claims and any consequent religious conflict.

Both 'no one will tell me what to do' and 'I am entitled to my own opinion' have become hallmarks of independent, free-thinking people in an age when the prevailing culture is a challenging mix of cultures, so 'the Bible says' cannot be regarded as a convincing and conclusive appeal to a supreme authority. Christianity is sometimes described as a religion of the book, and Christians have been called people of the book, but this is less true of Christianity than it is of most other world religions. The Christian faith is less book-centred than on first impression, for its doctrines allow for other authorities such as tradition, reason and experience to interplay with scripture in the formation of orthodox Christian faith. Through this quadrilateral of authorities – experience, reason, tradition and scripture – God reveals Godself to humankind, with the various Christian traditions giving priority to one or the other authority, often with democratising effect. Some Christians will say no one will tell me what to do because my experience suggests otherwise, while others will say I am entitled to my own opinions and logically I think such and such.

On the other hand, an ineradicable relationship exists between authorship and authority. The author of each and every novel mentioned in this book enjoys privilege over his or her offspring. This means that because the author is the origin of his or her work, the author is authoritative. This authority is ordinarily indicated by a symbol that carries much more weight than is implied by its unobtrusive placement on the page bearing publishing details – the copyright symbol, ©. When novelists place Bible stories and texts in their novels, the question of authority and authorship comes to the fore. Who has authored the texts they cite? Unlike the scriptures of many other faiths, we recognise that men (and probably no women) had a hand in writing, compiling, editing and interpreting the books of the Bible. Beyond, and inspiring, these human authors is, we might say, a divine author. God is the Author of authors who is behind and within the Book to which all books point. Thinking in this way about what the presence of Bible story and text does to fiction might lead us to say that God is the eternal transcendence signified by every book, not only the books of the Bible. Each book is a sign of God. Each bears God's signature, which is usually accepted as the hallmark of authority and authenticity. For this reason, as a literary scholar and theologian, or even merely as a Christian reader, I believe in literature.

Moreover, meaning in texts resides, not only on the page, but in several places – in the author's original intentions, in the reader's current responses and in the long tradition and many centuries of interpretation – and that meaning can, and does, change over time. How we read the

Bible is always changing, and is affected by time and culture as much as by contextual changes in our own lives. Since biblical scholarship and criticism has done its work, fewer people will allow themselves to read the Bible as pure history, inerrant theology or dictated divine words. Instead, we read it as a spiritual text, whose diverse documents, each in their own way, evoke a sense of divine presence and direct its readers into a close relationship with God. Its readers, however, always retain the privilege of choosing whether to believe it or not.[8] In other words, the authority of the Bible is not absolute; it depends on the reader attributing authority to its pages. Liturgically, Christians make this attribution when Bible readings in church are concluded with a declamation such as 'This is the word of the Lord', to which the congregation responds with either a confirming 'Amen' or an expression of thanks to God. This establishes a meaning-making, community-forming and authority-establishing pact between author and reader, the like of which is not necessarily peculiar to sacred texts. Overall, the use of sacred texts within novels makes a distinct border between sacred and secular texts even harder to find. Remarkably, secularity speaks of the holy and opens into the otherness of sacredness.

---

8. Ward, Keith, (2010), p. 150.

Chapter 3

SCIENCE FICTION

'Anything believed gains a measure of reality'[1]

'I believe in one God, the Father, the Almighty, maker of heaven and earth, of all that is, seen and unseen.' So begins the Nicene Creed, a creed common to most of Christendom and an indicator that religion and science fiction share common ground, for both explore the realms of the seen and the unseen. Both religious practice and science fiction ask what happens if the veil between the real and invisible worlds fray, so that we are able to see through from one to the other. We might therefore ask, from one point of view, what difference does our awareness of the world beyond make to the way we live in the imminent world? From the other, we might ask, what of the unseen can we experience in the visible world? Religious practice aims to lift practitioners, in worship and prayer, beyond the mundane into the transcendent, while science fiction aims to transport readers into other worlds either in the future or elsewhere in the galaxy.

At times, science fiction has appealed only to a niche market, some students of literature have been snooty about the genre and its readers have been regarded as geeks. Some science fiction has, therefore, been published without naming it as 'science fiction' so that the appeal of a new book has not been restricted to science fiction officianados. Some writers, most famously Margaret Atwood, have strongly resisted attempts to bring any of their novels under the science fiction banner. While Ursula Le Guin, in an article in *The Guardian* in July 2017, places Atwood's *The Handmaid's Tale* and the Maddaddam trilogy in science fiction as 'half prediction half satire', Atwood insists that they be categorised as speculative fiction. The word 'science' is the problem, in at least two respects. First, science is to do with 'knowledge', and Atwood is not showing the reader what she *knows* about future society, but what she speculates future society might be like if some of the trends she

1. Hrotic, *op. cit.*, p. 140.

discerns in contemporary society persist. Second, the use of the word science in SF raises the expectation that books will describe and discuss pioneering, cutting-edge technology, some of which is on the edge of possibility and some of which is beyond the possible. Readers are entitled to expect some science in the fiction. The indistinct boundary between science fiction and fantasy further complicates the task of definition. All this makes science fiction notoriously difficult to classify.

Take for instance G. Willow Wilson's debut novel, *Alif the Unseen* (2012), in which the narrator calculates that the unseen or incorporeal world is twice as great as what we can see and touch with our own eyes and hands, and which takes the reader through the veil between these worlds. It seems that nothing in the sales promotion of this novel associated it with the world of science fiction, so this discussion must begin by assessing its SF credentials. Wilson's novel crosses into several worlds – the world of computer programming and its hacking underworld, the political world of the 2011 Arab spring, the fantasy world of *djinns* and genies known to us through *Arabian Nights*, the political and theological world of Islam with its clash between modernity and antiquity, and the seen and unseen worlds. The eponymous Alif is himself caught between two worlds: as the son of an absent Arab father and an Indian mother, he doesn't quite fit in the hierarchy of Muslim society. The location of the novel's events is a fictional city on the old Silk Road, never named, but always referred to as the City. It is a liminal place where the earthly world meets the Empty Quarter, the domain of ghouls and *ifrit* who can transmogrify into all manner of bestial shapes. Interweaving the worldviews of the mosque, political revolution, the computer underworld and the legends of *Arabian Nights*, Wilson takes Alif, as a fugitive in both the corporeal and incorporeal realms, on an adventure that brings these worlds together. All these worlds are clearly Muslim worlds. With the pace of a thriller, the romance of Arabian fantasy and magical realism elements including walls that people can walk through to reach the Immovable Alley, *Alif the Unseen* also bears a deep and detailed interest in computers and depicts some powerful and dangerous alien creatures from a fantasy world. The book was deservedly among the 2013 finalists for a major science fiction prize, the John W. Campbell Award.

Until the novel opens, Alif has earned an amoral living as a hacker giving online protection from censorious authorities to a range of nefarious users of the worldwide web. When he devises a computer program capable of identifying users from the pattern of their typing rhythm as they enter text on the screen, he finds he can no longer remain anonymous and hidden, especially when a notorious state censor known as The Hand of God stamps down on illicit computer activity. At the same time Intisar, his lover who is taken away from Alif into an arranged marriage, sends him as a parting gift an old book entitled *A Thousand and One Days*. Narrated by Islamic spirits, this book contains all their secrets and stories. His chief adversary in the world of computer hacking, The Hand, covets this beautiful and rare masterpiece, as he believes it also contains the key to making the leap from binary to quantum computing. Alif is forced to flee, weaving in and out of real and irreal worlds to escape The Hand. At one stage, he endures brutal treatment for months in a dark, airless and isolated cell, almost dying there, and hallucinating as he moves in and out of the imagined interior world in his head and the filthy prison cell external to his body. His allies include a ferocious *djinn*, an elderly imam, a renegade Gulf prince, a pious niqab-wearing neighbour called Dina, and a young American woman never named, but referred to throughout as 'the convert'. The novelist, too, is a young American convert to Islam. In people like these, different worlds converge, and one world enlightens another. For instance, the imam intuitively, but unexpectedly, understands Alif's explanation of quantum computing because he recalls that it is said that each word of the Qur'ān has 7,000 layers of meaning each of which, although seemingly transgressive or unfathomable, exists equally at all times without ultimate contradiction. These are witty links between two apparently quite unrelated worlds, those of computer science and scriptural hermeneutics.

What distinguishes *Alif the Unseen* from most novels in this study is that its setting is Islamic. Its world is politically, mythologically, theologically and morally Muslim. Wilson has set Alif's adventure among the religious figures, the uneasy politics, and the fantastic creatures of Arab society, and demonstrated that religious belief (in this case, Muslim belief) is flexible and multi-faceted enough to slip into different human settings. Not all characters in the novel believe this: one unnamed man, who is unable to help Alif rescue Dina and the convert from danger, is more critical of organised religion and says, 'Belief . . . doesn't mean the same thing it used to, not for you. You have unlearned the hidden half of the world.'

Alif protests,

> But the world is crawling with religious fanatics. Surely belief is thriving.
>
> Superstition is thriving. Pedantry is thriving. Sectarianism is thriving. Belief is dying out. To most of your people the djinn are paranoid fantasies who run around causing epilepsy

and mental illness. Find me someone to whom the hidden folk are simply real, as described in the Books. You'll be searching a long time. Wonder and awe have gone out of your religions. You are prepared to accept the irrational, but not the transcendent. And that, cousin, is why I can't help you (299).

Although this criticism in the context of the novel is levelled at Islam, it could also be said of other faiths, including Christianity. Indeed, the book can be read as a critique of any organised religion.

Insights in *Alif the Unseen* might also be true of contemporary Christianity. Prompted by this novel we might ask, 'Has transcendence been lost in our religious practices?' What contribution does the popular notion of guardian angels make to the overall picture of Christianity, and how does it relate to the stories of *djinn* and genies? Where is the crossover from theology to superstition? How do we lift the curtain to see through into the unseen? And, noting that there is an interesting ongoing relationship between the Qur'ān and *One Thousand and One Days* in the novel, is there a similar relationship between the Christian Bible and other literature such as Milton's *Paradise Lost* or Dante's *Inferno*?

According to Adam Roberts, the roots of science fiction reach deeper into the soil of world literature than is often accepted.[2] Brian Aldiss traced its origins back to Mary Shelley's *Frankenstein,* Thomas Disch to Edgar Allan Poe, Patrick Parrinder to H.G. Wells and Jules Verne, and Samuel Delaney traced it back no further than 1926 when Hugo Gernsback coined the term. But Roberts finds its roots as deep in literary history as the fantastic voyages of the ancient Greek novel. Both science fiction and these ancient texts tell of *voyages extraordinaire* (to use the phrase Roberts borrows from Jules Verne), and they have a shared interest in the technology of travel. In the case of science fiction these extraordinary voyages are journeys through time and space, whether upwards to other planets or deeper into Earth, while in the case of the Greek epic they are sea adventures to locations such as the Gates of Herakles.

Throughout its history, science fiction has been interested in the role of religion. Several critics have examined how an almost symbiotic relationship has developed in the twentieth- and twenty-first centuries, during a period when the common assumption is that religion and science are dichotomous. These critical examinations include Tom Woodman's study of transcendence in science fiction in Longman's 1979 critical guide to the genre, Farah Mendlesohn's chapter in the 2003 *Cambridge*

2. Roberts, (2016), pp. vii and xv.

Companion to Science Fiction, James McGrath's 2012 study of religion and science fiction for Lutterworth Press and Steven Hrotic's *Religion in Science Fiction* for Bloomsbury in 2016. Hrotic demarcates six distinct eras in which the relationship between religion and science fiction varied. In the 1920s, religion in science fiction tended to be no more than a supportive thread to the main plot, although it was a remarkably frequent thread. Religion was often associated with unenlightened societies, its practitioners were often manipulative and dishonest and there were few who lay outside the mainstream. Then, in the late 1930s and early 1940s, religion was cast in SF as being based on misunderstandings about the world, society and history, and some writers of the time began to question the inevitability of religion in human societies. After 1945, the science fiction community struggled to come to terms with the impact and the implications of the atomic bomb, and religion remained a potent social tool in science fiction. Although religion in science fiction continued to be antagonistic to science, the tension was less absolute than previously. In the 1960s, religion in science fiction was neither entirely positive nor negative, but simply a force of nature that could not be ignored if we want to understand human beings and their societies. In the following decade, religion was usually interpreted by science fiction as potentially benevolent, though it was often held at arm's length. In the science fiction of the final decades of the twentieth century, religion was seen to have social value especially if it was flexible and capable of evolution. In this most recent era, religions were often invented for the imagined worlds of the novels and faith became a valued concept.

Clearly, science fiction provides scope both to consider the role of religion in any future or contemporary society and to speculate what society might more generally be like in the future, and we can see from Hrotic's analysis that the relationship between religion and science fiction has been symbiotic. The crux of the relationship lies both in the fact that 'anything believed, even fictional worlds, gain [*sic*] a measure of reality'[3] and in the strangeness and ultimate knowability of the universe, towards an understanding of which the multiplicity of religious worldviews carries the human race.[4]

Filmed and televised science fiction is outside the scope of this book. However, it is readily accessible, and there are many who watch science fiction, but who would not choose to read it. We should, therefore, note that long-running series such as the BBC's *Dr Who*, in which the time-travelling and space-hopping Doctor is reincarnated in various forms,

3. Hrotic, *op. cit.*, p. 140.
4. *ibid.* p. 199.

often discuss theological, religious and spiritual themes, and American series such as *Star Trek*, which has no specific religious content and is usually presumed to be entirely secular, can be subject to theological study.[5]

Chris Beckett's four science fiction novels, to date, provide an interesting contemporary example of religious themes in the genre. The first, *The Holy Machine* – published in America in 2004, but not until 2011 in the UK – after Beckett had worked a long apprenticeship writing short stories, is set in Illyria that had been founded as a refuge from twenty-first-century fundamentalist religion. Its very title draws attention to the novel's mix of sacredness and science. However, the novel's protagonist, George Simling, finds Illyria's militant rationalism as repressive as the aggressive religion he had experienced elsewhere. Now, having fallen in love with a syntec, a machine built for sex with perfect looks and human skin who has begun to develop conscious sentience, George sees that his only option is to leave Illyria and head for the Outlands. There, however, robots are in danger of death.

Before leaving, he meets religious believers within Illyria for the first time. These are Janine and Yussef who both share three beliefs – in God, in a book as the infallible word of God and in a man who long ago had been God's spokesperson on earth. However, the books and the men are different, for one was Muslim, the other Christian. Because Janine was of a similar age and background as himself, George listens more attentively to what she says. She expresses an Ignatian view of the world as a vale of tears, a soul-making world preparing people for eternity, one's experience of which varied depending upon whether or not one acknowledged Christ as Saviour. George is familiar with this notion as he had heard similar ideas from a priest in former days. The convention in Illyria was that religion was ignorant and savage; George found Janine's expression of her faith disappointing. The notion that one's ultimate destiny depended on how one responded to the life of one man who had lived 2,000 years previously seemed arbitrary and repellent in its intolerance of alternative belief systems. 'Janine's religion had taken mystery and reduced it to a kind of inexorable machine' (114).

Significantly, the main protest group in Illyria is known as the Army of the Human Spirit and is portrayed on TV as 'a bunch of religious fanatics' (104). However, its manifesto expresses its aims more moderately. Fundamental to the group's belief is the expectation that the human spirit cannot thrive in any environment when only that which can be measured is acknowledged as real. Humanity requires a sense

5. See Neece, (2018).

of an unseen world beyond whatever meets the eye, so the Army of the Human Spirit seeks freedom of religious and artistic expression and an end to the mechanisation of humanity and the programme of systematically substituting robots for human beings. The strength of the religious themes and the abundance of religious ideas in Beckett's first novel set the tone for the trilogy that followed, the first of which, *Dark Eden*, was awarded the 2013 Arthur C. Clarke Award for the best science fiction novel published in Britain in the previous year. The stature of the first recipient in 1988 – Margaret Atwood for *The Handmaid's Tale* – indicates the prestige of this prize.

Six generations before the events narrated in *Dark Eden*, two astronauts had been marooned on an eerie non-solar planet. Since then, inbreeding had resulted in a number of their descendants suffering cleft palettes and lameness. These are derided as batfaces and clawfeet. By this stage in the colonisation of Eden, the community has developed an ancestor-worship mythology whose focal centre is a Circle of Stones, placed where the astronauts originally landed and from where the inhabitants now believe Earth will rescue them (36-7). Despite a decadent sexual morality in which sexual intercourse is simply called 'slipping', women are reduced to mere sex objects to provide male relief, and pregnancies and birth are like factory production lines, religious ritual has an important role in this society. The novel represents an inversion of the Christian metanarrative in which humankind has been alienated and exiled from the primaeval and paradisiacal Eden, and hopes either to return there from fallen Earth or to re-establish Eden on Earth; in *Dark Eden,* the people of Eden wait to return to Earth (61). An annual ceremony, known in the debased form of language resulting from years of separation from other native speakers as the Any Versry, includes a rehearsal of their creation story cherishing the inhabitants' links with their ancestors and their history, and is reminiscent of the Christian liturgy's repeated rehearsal of its creation and redemption narrative in the Eucharistic prayer and denominational attachments to founding fathers (77 and 79). The story is re-enacted in the manner of a passion play (122-34), and both the development of a liturgy and the presence of a strict moral code formalises the story's role among the stranded humans as a community-forming religion (117).

John, a young man described by Stuart Kelly in *The Guardian* review of the novel as 'a mix of Prometheus, Moses and Gilgamesh', becomes a thorn in the side of the Eden community. His desire to roam further across the planet is strongly resisted by the others who want always to be near the Circle of Stones in readiness for their rescue (116). But John is a reformer who has found Angela's talismanic ring that she had lost soon after she arrived on Eden (111). She and the others who had ventured out from Earth so long ago had been spurred by a sense that Jesus wanted humankind to cross over Starry Swirl and find new worlds (123). Now John Redlantern wants to break out, too. The novel explores how society deals with disruptive reform movements like John's (137). Although it feels like an act of sacrilege to break up the Circle of Stones, the impulse to do so cannot be resisted (145) and the circle is pulled apart. Community cohesion is undoubtedly disrupted in such a way that social and moral stability breaks down. The disturbance of the community's norms is beyond recovery when three Family members raid John's new settlement, attack Jeff and attempt to rape Tina. When the raiders are resisted and killed, these are the first murders on Eden, and John decides they must go further across Snowy Dark.

When his leadership is called into question, John uses the ring as a bargaining tool, but exaggerates its significance by implying that, rather than simply finding a lost ring, a resurrected Christ-like apparition of Angela had visited him and shown him where the ring could be found (267). So, when the community next re-enacts the loss of the ring episode in their storytelling, John accordingly changes the ending (265). This is a telling change: story is central to religion and the story is ever-developing. Having a 'story that carries on' (311) is vital, and not to have one is sad and socially destructive. However, to encourage others to accept and follow his heterodox behaviour, John fabricates a story in which Gela gives him direct instructions: 'she told me she wanted us to spread out over Eden, and find new places to live, and new hunting grounds. She *told* me' (306). Not all of his companions trust John's claims. One remembers that the original explorers from Earth had claimed that 'Jesus Juice . . . whoever Jesus was' had encouraged space exploration, and another enigmatically comments on John's leadership: 'Claiming to get instructions from some old dead person. Now what does that remind me of?' (306). Because the Edenfolk show little evidence of accurately remembering anything of Christian beliefs or practice, I suspect that this enigmatic comment indicates the author's own critique of Christianity, its claim on truth and authority, and its role in the formation of human society.

Eventually the breakaway group under John's leadership enters a new world, a wide forest with all the space they could possibly need for many generations to come, which they call Wide Forest (336). The group left behind clears up the damage done by John's rebels, but the new circle of stones cannot replace the originals. With hindsight they wonder whether they should have 'spiked that John up like Jesus' (344).

Later, John's breakaway group finds the crashed Landing Veekle with the skeletons of Mehmet, Dixon and Michael (386), confirming the old story that they had believed was true, but had not really believed happened in the same world as theirs (387). History thus becomes part of their present; the remembered is actualised.

Dark Eden concludes with a deep sense that Eden can never be good, as one of those left behind, Sue Redlantern, curses the first Tommy, Dixon and Mehmet for bringing human life to Eden and the first Tommy and Angela for 'slipping' together and perpetuating human existence: 'bringing everyone from peaceful nothingness into this cruel dark world. . . . Nothing good would ever come to us in this miserable dark Eden' (394). Yet it is plain that there is no way back. John Redlantern, standing beside the Landing Veekle, tells his companions that he now realises that the spaceship that they had for generations believed had returned to Earth to bring help had, in fact, never left Eden. No call for help had been made and hope of Earth was now lost to them. Tearfully, they wail, 'That means they'll never come for us' (399). On the other hand, it does mean that these three ancestors are back in Eden's story, so John and his friends take the astronauts' bones and drop them into the deep waterforest of Worldpool (402). As they say goodbye to Earth to which they can never return, Angela's totemic ring becomes the most precious thing left (403) and the story has changed once more.

The second instalment, *Mother of Eden* (2015), narrates events 400 years after the crash and, as Kelly says in his review, continues to explore how foundation stories mutate and form distinctive linguistic worlds. Now that the Eden community has been sundered and enmity exists between the Johnfolk and the Davidfolk, the stories told among those who remained faithful to the original community are now presented as puppet shows demonising John Redlantern (56). Angela's ring does not carry universal high regard; indeed, 'it's just a ring' (19), although the Veeklehouse where the Landing Veekl had been discovered has acquired shrine-like status among the traders (30-2). Society has become predatory. Forgery of the stick currency is countered by brutal punishment. If science fiction is fiction without science, then these books take it one step further. In the Eden trilogy, science has been forgotten, once-civilised people have descended into ignorance and misunderstanding, and technological civilisation has been left behind.

However, the ring becomes a symbol of healing (308-9), and once Starlight returns with the ring it attracts new stories because storytelling built on old stories cannot be resisted (428). When Starlight mysteriously disappears, Julie fabricates a tale of finding the ring on a dead woman when they were being chased by New Earth people (433). However, Julie catches up with Starlight, who has not died as readers thought, and they reach Half Sky, where three people carrying spears cautiously welcome them (450). Later, evangelists tell stories of Starlight as a healer (464), though Quietstream Batwing does not recognise the Starlight she knew in these stories (465). Perhaps as a 'resurrected' healer, thought to have died, but not actually having done so, Starlight represents, to some extent, a Christ figure. Indeed, Quietstream's failure to recognise her is reminiscent of the New Testament accounts of the risen Christ.

The finale of the trilogy, *Daughter of Eden* (2016), switches the expectations of disappointment at the end of volume one and throughout the second volume, and asks what would happen to a society such as Eden's if its messianic hopes were in fact fulfilled. When the prophecies come true in this novel, can the mythology Edenfolk have developed and the stories they have told still survive? In *Daughter of Eden*, Earth dwellers, on an expedition to see what they can learn of Eden (258), return to the eerie planet from which, for centuries, the descendants of the original explorers had longed for rescue (178).

What has prevailed throughout all three novels is an exploration of what it means to be at home. Religion, too, often has an interest in the concept of home. 'Everyone needs a home,' says Angie Redlantern who narrates *Daughter of Eden*. When men like John Redlantern turn their backs on their homes, they are seeking a better home – deeper, stronger and truer than the flimsy homes others cling to. Angie opines that, as we are merely passing through this world, the impermanence of home is unsettling; we never feel properly or truly at home. She recommends that her fellow citizens of Eden should listen out for Mother, then one day they will go to their true home, either by starship, if they are still alive when Earth returns for them, or their 'shadows will fly there after [they] are dead' (42). Earth is as warm and bright, and as beckoning and redolent of ultimate happiness for the characters in these novels as heaven is for Christians.

In the early chapters of *Daughters of Eden*, a theology develops that builds on the ancestor worship and mythology of the first novels, for teachers start to understand and set down that the president, their ancestral founder who had sent astronauts to Eden in the first place and whom readers assumed was the president of the United States, had been there from the beginning and had made Eden, the Earth and all the stars. He was more than just a man (74). This does not displace ancestor worship: mounds of stones piled over graves fill Burial Grounds for the dead. The clearing with these Burial Mounds became 'a peaceful little

world all on its own' (145) where the scale of Angela (Gela) Young's
grave that dwarfed all others showed how she was still reaching out
to others, pouring out her love and making herself heard. Angie is
frustrated, though, that Gela does not speak to her as she does to Mary:
how like the young evangelical churchgoer who yearns to know God as
intimately as others seem to do!

As in *Dark Eden*, Beckett explores the role of story, initially arguing
that stories help us make the best of things:

> They were so important we told them to ourselves in our
> heads, every time we went to sleep. They were how we joined
> together all the things that happened to us into a shape that
> made some kind of sense. They were how we made the best of
> things in this sad, lonely place, where babies can burn up with
> fever, and enemies can come across the water, and people can
> be born with clawfeet and batfaces, and be teased and left out,
> and can't do anything about it. (155)

Such stories are subconscious as dreams and conscious as religious
fables, myths, creeds and liturgies. They can be controverted: the Story
told throughout the trilogy had said that the president was a woman,
but after Earth's arrival on Eden they learn that they had mistakenly
conflated two historical figures, the male president of Merka and Kate
Grantham, the Drekter of the Glacksy Project. Disturbingly, true history
unravels their stories (291), but uncertainty need not limit the value of
story, and Angie reflects that the best anyone can do is 'think about the
people and the situation [they] are in, and figure out for [oneself] what
makes most sense' (355). There would be no stories if we only told those
we were totally certain about, for no one can fully trust his or her own
memories (356). Edenfolk learn from their conversation with Earthfolk
that the narrative of a belief system gives access to truth, but that there
are as many forms of, or perspectives on, truth as there are stories. Within
these novels, the stories, though compromised and eternally evolving, are
truth-telling as well as community-forming. That there is also a Secret
Story whose telling is forbidden on Eden suggests the power of story to
control. Indeed, Starlight was killed for telling this Secret Story (97).
Keeping secret the Secret Story – that black people are as good as white
people and that women are as good as men – retains the social inequalities
those in power do not want to lose (343). Although the Earth people
had shown the Edenfolk the light, when the spaceship lifts off to return
to Earth with its three Earth people and the only one Eden person there

was room for, the narrator judges that they were no more enlightened: they were still where they had always been – on dark, dark Eden (367). The era-marking event of Earth's return to Eden means that things can never be the same again and the stories must change, even though 'so many people depend on them in so many different ways' (258). Some of the changes are necessitated by the unfamiliar technology the Earth people brought with them, and this reminds me of the troubling effects of science and the rational mind on the narratives of Christianity. To say God made us, the world and everything that is in it means something quite different in a post-Galileo, post-Darwin and post-Hume age. The story has shifted, but the changes in the way the story is told do not invalidate it. The story told by the Edenfolk in Beckett's trilogy has a different tone, too. It is nonetheless a story making a home for its tellers.

Why is there such interest in religion in Beckett's work? As a former social worker now working as an academic teaching social work at the University of East Anglia, Beckett must be aware of the role of religion as a sociological phenomenon. His main interest in these novels is the formation of human communities. He takes the Edenfolk back to their origins in two people marooned on Eden and watches how their new, isolated society forms and collapses under strain. He observes the development of religious story, religious practice and spiritual behaviour. The foundation stories the characters tell each other bring together the community and create new mythology.

Thus, the Eden trilogy raises several significant questions for thinking Christians who read the novels. First, Beckett quickly established in the trilogy that the displaced humans develop a different moral code, and I find myself asking whether a slip in morality is an inevitable consequence of dislocation. One should be careful here, for it is easy to fall into the fallacy of assuming that morality is intrinsically and exclusively religious. Those who do not hold a religious worldview live by an ethical code, too!

Second, ancestor worship, expressed in the regular rehearsal of the story of the origins of the human community on Eden, helps bind the community together, for example in *Dark Eden* (122-34). I wonder how this compares with both the cult of saints that developed within Christianity and our modern awareness of our religious heritage and our spiritual forebears. How does this relate to what St Paul says about the tradition he handed on? There are points of comparison between Eden's ancestor worship and the Christian 'remembering' at Holy Communion.

John embellishes his discovery of Angela's lost ring into an 'untruthful' account of an apparition of Angela showing him where it could be found. Would this apparition, if it had actually occurred, have been comparable to the New Testament accounts of the appearances of the resurrected Christ? If so, does this destabilise our trust in, and our use of, these accounts? Does the unhistorical, but theological, embellishment of the Easter narratives in the Gospels compromise them, in current times, as evidence for Christ's resurrection?

In *Dark Eden* (265), John makes further changes to the foundational narrative. Clearly, the story, although central to their belief, is subject to change. The Christian narrative, the Gospel story, is similarly ever-developing on the basis of new knowledge, fresh insights and changes in language. It is the old, old story, but told ever anew for each generation. We should consider which takes precedence: does the change of belief amend the story, or does change in the story alter what is believed?

In *Mother of Eden*, Starlight had been presumed dead and, after she was discovered to be still alive, stories were told about her as a healer. On Starlight's return, however, Quietstream Batwing fails to recognise her. If Starlight serves as a Christ figure in the novel, then her unrecognisability is reminiscent of the New Testament accounts of the risen Christ. I am struck by the question of the recognisability of Jesus. Would those who had known him in Nazareth and Galilee have recognised his depiction by the Gospel writers in the New Testament? Would they recognise his depiction by the Church throughout the ages? And where do we see Jesus now? Would we simply walk by if Jesus came to Birmingham, as Geoffrey Studdert Kennedy famously asked in his war-time poem?

One of the trilogy's recurring themes is that of home. Although the humans long to return home to Earth, they must make homes on Eden and seek better homes. Much hymnody of the 200 years has suggested that this world is not our home, we are simply passing through and the process of dying has been likened to going home. As a result, the longing for home described in these novels chimes in with the traditional Christian hope for heaven.

The final theological theme of these books is story. Beckett is telling a story of people who are themselves storytellers. Newly discovered truths can unravel stories, but uncertainty need not close down the story or silence the storyteller. The trilogy concludes with the notion that the best we can do is think about ourselves and our circumstances and tell the story of ourselves that makes the most sense (*Daughter of Eden*, 355). Indeed, if we only told stories we were certain about, we would tell none. This raises in my mind a question about how we tell Bible stories, and in what sense they are *our* stories, if we were not there. They become our stories because we originate in them, we find our place in them and we find our fulfilment in them.

Any novel that uses phrases from a petition in the Lord's Prayer as titles for its four constituent parts – Part 1 'Thy Will Be Done', Part 2 'On Earth', Part 3 'As it is' and Part 4 'In Heaven' – must be presenting itself as a religious novel, yet the author of *The Book of Strange New Things*, Michel Faber, is an atheist, the novel is undoubtedly a story of space travel and the book can readily be classified as science fiction (though not advertised as such). The eponymous book of strange new things is the Christian Bible and the purpose of the space travel within the novel is to evangelise the alien inhabitants of a distant planet, so a more specifically religious example of science fiction would be difficult to find. Faber's publications have often shown interest in either religion or the fantastic: his first novel, *Under the Skin* (2000), tells of a surgically transformed woman from an unidentified alien territory who abducts hitchhikers to export them back to her birthplace as food, while his 2009 novella, *The Fire Gospel*, tells of a scholar's discovery of a fifth long-forgotten Gospel purportedly written by Malchus. *The Book of Strange New Things* combines both his interests. In a review in *The Independent*, Hannah McGill greets this novel as genre-defying – neither sci-fi, speculative fiction nor literary fiction – but simply a book to be welcomed as 'Never before now'. However, the book falls neatly into a subgenre of the Golden Age of science fiction in which books such as Mary Doria Russell's *The Sparrow* or James Blish's *A Case of Conscience* tell of missionaries going to aliens, either to liberate or enthral them.

Yet *The Book of Strange New Things* is more than a missionary story. It begins with an account of fumbled and awkward sex in a car outside an airport as Peter and his wife, Bea, bid each other farewell, before Peter flies away to the distant planet of Oasis to serve as a missionary. Their continuing relationship, carried out by nothing other than written correspondence by means of interplanetary email, forms the central interest of the novel. Their letters are full of heart-breaking conversations, made all the more tear-jerking because they often cover the mundane matters that populate the conversations between many married couples who, unlike Peter and Bea permanently living on different planets, share the same home. As they struggle to understand each other's new lives, Bea becomes increasingly angry and desperate, while Peter loses interest in her less fascinating earthly existence. Nevertheless, the loneliness each feels because of the separation never eases: they often write of believing that they belong together, by each other's side, and his last, baseless words to her are 'Don't give up. I will find you.'

Peter, who had first met Bea when she nursed him after breaking both his ankles, had served as pastor of a small church in England before being recruited by a global missionary organisation, known only as USIC, to replace a missionary who has mysteriously disappeared from the human settlement on Oasis. He and Bea, as obedient Christians, accept the necessary separation as the cost of God's calling.

The Book of Strange New Things addresses several questions including colonialism, translation between languages and the nature of Christian mission. Faber presents Peter and Bea's Christian faith seriously and does not mock it in any way. Their religion is sincere and without duplicity. Because he does not present them as unscrupulous Christians, but as people who genuinely want to be faithful to God and improve the lot of their fellows, Faber enables his readers to ask serious questions of a serious faith. That is not to say that the book lacks any element of religious satire. Readers cannot avoid asking searching questions about the ethics of colonialism. A story of humans populating and proselytising a distant planet inevitably reminds us of Europeans taking Christianity to Africa, Asia and the Americas. Questions about the history of colonialism, its use and abuse of fellow creatures, and the manner in which aggressive land grabs were accompanied by missionaries preaching Christianity, cannot be far from readers' minds.

The book raises contemporary questions, too. Trade between humans and Oasans is limited to food produced by the natives for the human settlement in return for which Oasans are content to receive painkillers and the 'book of strange new things'. What it will be like in the future is not clear because USIC is building an infrastructure to support a larger population. However, the term 'colony' is studiously avoided in preference for 'community' or 'partnership'. This raises a question of language that is related to one of the main difficulties Peter faces as a missionary: how to communicate the tropes of his religion to an alien culture. Accounts of Oasans pummelling local plants and insects and using them as dyes to make meals resembling Earth food raise questions about food farming in the real modern world. For instance, nations where people are starving, supply specialist baby vegetables to European supermarkets, and food growers in Britain often depend on seasonal migrant workers travelling from the other side of Europe to do back-breaking work for minimum wages. We are led to ask whether real people on Earth – both former colonialists and contemporary so-called partners – are any better than the human settlers on Faber's Oasis?

The matter of translation from one language to another poses a problem for any science fiction writer telling stories of encounters with alien species. The Oasans are hungry for the Gospel and Peter must take a ready-translated text. Consonant sounds the Oasans are unable to pronounce, which Faber represents on the page with invented letters, have been removed from the Bible Peter takes with him, as have all references to images, such as sheep, with which the Oasans could never relate. These problems of translation and meaning on the fictional planet have also been encountered in real life in recent centuries. For instance, Bible translators have had to weigh up how much consideration should be given to the author's original intended meaning and how much should be given to how meaning can be conveyed in today's terminology. The Church continues to wrestle with the limits of language, not only in its inability to define (or, indeed, get anywhere near defining) God, but also in the worldview assumptions that lie behind the language we use. In this regard, we might note that we hamper ourselves when we continue to use the 'up' and 'down' language of heaven and earth at the Feast of the Ascension of Christ, although we are helped out by the fact that much of this language is retained elsewhere such as in schools where pupils go up a class. In this novel, Peter and Bea's relationship is conducted entirely through words on a page, and readers will be aware that words on a page are more open to misreading than words spoken by a person whose inflexion can be heard and whose expression can be seen. If, therefore, words are all we use to communicate, how do changes in words, especially in translation, affect meaning? One of the difficulties about describing our beliefs to others is that of knowing whether what we say has been understood by someone else when his or her experience of words might be radically, or even subtly, different. This missionary problem for Peter on Oasis is the modern church's problems of biblical and theological interpretation and apologetics: how do we express our faith to people whose native tongue is not theological?

The Book of Strange New Things can be seen as an examination of dislocation – Peter is separated from his earth-bound wife, Bea, earthlings live in a sealed bubble on Oasis and Peter's relationship with the aliens is often troubled – but it also meditates on the capacity of either love or faith to endure the extreme pressure of such dislocation. The novel challenges Christianity's evangelical enterprise in a period of human history when we are closer than we ever have been to people of other faiths and none. When Christians living, working and worshipping in any British city in the early decades of the twenty-first century meet Muslims, Hindus, Sikhs and Buddhists on a daily basis, what goals can there be for evangelism and what is the nature of Christian mission? How has the Church's mission changed? Indeed, has it ever been appropriate to convert people from indigenous religion?

Church is a place for asking questions, for by letting our curious selves ask challenging questions, we learn, grow and mature towards fuller understanding of the seen and unseen. Novel-reading Christians probably know this already, for they are explorers. Both science fiction and religion, by enabling us to imagine other worlds and by teaching us to ask questions, offer the means to make a different future.

Chapter 4

DYSTOPIA AND FANTASY
'Books with magic and books without'

In the twentieth century, fantasy was a vibrant genre of religious writing for children. Authors such as C.S. Lewis and Elizabeth Goudge, who built on the tradition of religious fantasy established by George MacDonald, and their less well-known successors, Alan Garner and Susan Cooper, wrote within this genre. Philip Pullman and J.K. Rowling, both of whom are much less committed to the Christian worldview than Lewis, yet whose novels depend as much on aspects of Christian mythology and carry spiritual themes, have re-energised the fantasy genre for children in recent years. Many adults also enjoy reading children's fantasy and this has spilt over to create a thirst among adult readers for fantasy fiction. J.R.R. Tolkien, Terry Pratchett and Neil Gaiman enjoy cult followings. In addition to these written texts, film and television shows including series such as Game of Thrones, Harry Potter, the Hunger Games, and Marvel and DC superhero stories have created a high level of familiarity with fantasy fiction in both its dark dystopic form and its rosier utopic form.

You might ask, 'What has God to do with fantasy fiction?' And you might think, not much. Yet many imagined fantasy worlds allude to religion in the rituals their creators invent for their inhabitants, as well as in the presence of a divine or supernatural being as a fantastic creature. For a very recent example, Gareth Hanrahan's dark fantasy entitled *The Gutter Prayer* includes vengeful gods, terrifying hallucinations and out-of-body experiences, alongside monsters and magic.

Close correlation between religion and fantasy literature is almost inevitable, for Christianity has always imagined an end time. Old Testament prophets spoke of a Day of the Lord and the New Testament spoke of an ultimate Day of Judgement. Some expect a Day of Judgement when they die; other Christians believe the Day of Judgment comes later, after a time of sleep in death while waiting for the last trumpet to sound, a scene scarily and effectively depicted in Michelangelo's Sistine Chapel painting. Requiem Masses portray this as a *Dies Irae*, a Day of Wrath. End time theology, known as eschatology, was not only about the ultimate destinies of individual souls, but also about an actual end time when all that is known to us comes to a final conclusion, an apocalypse. Millenarianist groups at various moments in Christian history have gathered in expectation of the end of the world, usually ill-prepared for the disappointment they were about to face, and forced to revise the date of their expectation. However, for the last sixty or seventy years, we have lived in an age when we can, for the first time, actually see how the end time might occur. The world is now much more interconnected than ever before. What happens in a once remote corner of the world can have immediate impact elsewhere in the world. The internet draws us closer together and makes the world smaller. One does not have to be a doom-monger to suggest that nuclear warfare, cyber failure such as the feared Y2K millennium bug or malevolent cyberattacks, and climate change causing extreme weather and rendering tracts of land inhospitable could easily be the means by which the four horsemen of the apocalypse ride into town heralding the end time. Imagining the collapse of human civilisation into dystopic visions thus requires relatively little effort.

In their study of fantasy fiction for children, Michael Levy and Farah Mendlesohn defined fantasy fiction as the realisation of the impossible.[1] Mendlesohn identified four modes of fantasy: the portal quest in which a fantastic world is entered through some form of doorway or passage and the tale is told like a tourist account; the intrusion fantasy where a fantastic otherworld intrudes upon, disrupts and defeats the normative world; the immersive fantasy where the imagined fantasy world is simply the normative world of the protagonists without any explanation to readers in the real world; and liminal fantasies where readers and protagonist do not agree which world is fantasy and which is normative, making readers doubt the dominant voice in the narrative. I suggest that in many respects this puts fantasy fiction on the same ground as religion. Both are to do with two worlds, the real and the irreal, earth and heaven, the physical and the spiritual realms, what we have and what we hope for. Both fantasy fiction and religion are to do with the interface of these two worlds and the crossover between them. Fantasy fiction is sometimes dismissed as a form of escapism. And yet, escapism is not a sin in the writing or reading of literature. Visiting alternative places – Hogwarts, Narnia or Middle Earth – can be pleasurable. Other fantastic places – Gormenghast, Westeros and Hansel and Gretel's wood, for

1. Levy and Mendlesohn, (2016), p. 3.

instance – are thoroughly unattractive places to visit. Yet our visits to these alternate worlds, whether pleasant or not, offer respite when we are feeling the ill effects of life in the real world. They provide space to accommodate the adjustments we might need to make to flourish in the real world. This renders allegedly escapist fantasy actually non-escapist. Levy and Mendlesohn claim that children are enabled to face up to serious life issues when reading fantasy fiction because such issues are less threatening when they have been removed from the real world.[2] In fantasy, they can face demons. What they claim for children applies to adults, too. Fantasy fiction provides a safe place for readers of any age to face whatever troubles or perplexes them.

I choose to take what may seem an unorthodox step in this chapter. I will discuss fantasy and dystopia as one, for we might think of fantasy and dystopia not as two distinct genres, but simply as two facets of the same genre: 'books with magic and books without'. Some fantasies are utopias; others are set in dystopic worlds. Some are uplifting, enlightening and joyous; others are what David Mitchell in *The Bone Clocks* (2014) called 'Endarkenment'. Among earliest canonical and non-canonical Christian writings, apocalyptic literature was akin to modern-day fantasy. The term apocalyptic means revelatory. Apocalyptic literature, therefore, uncovers what was previously hidden and unveils truth. So the mission I choose to take up in this chapter is to uncover godly truth within secular fantasy literature of the twenty-first century.

John Bunyan's *Pilgrim's Progress*, the fantastic, allegorical and archetypal spiritual biography, which was placed alongside the Bible both on the bookshelves and in the ethos of my Protestant childhood home, links many of the novels discussed in this chapter. Like *Pilgrim's Progress*, Cormac McCarthy's *The Road* (2006) recounts a pilgrimage from a place, to which return is impossible, towards a hoped-for happier land; Andrew Michael Hurley's *The Loney* (2014) references the Protestant *Pilgrim's Progress* while its focus is on a Catholic parish's Holy Week retreat to a remote coastline away from the streets of London; and Alan Moore, who supplies a foreword to the 2012 edition of B. Catling's *The Vorrh* (2007), identifies *Pilgrim's Progress* as the foundation text for all modern fantasy writing. Vanity Fair and the Slough of Despond are among the dystopias in *Pilgrim's Progress*; Beulah is its ultimate fantasy land.

Public awareness of Cormac McCarthy's dystopic novel *The Road* increased after the release of John Hillcoat's film of the book in 2009. The novel depicts a 'barren, silent, godless' America, across which a

2. *ibid.*, p. 225.

father and his son travel south from their ruined home in an expectation, based on no real evidence, that they will find a better home. The terrain they cross has been devastated by a catastrophe that has rendered the scene apocalyptic and left human society in tatters. Intentionally reminiscent of Bunyan's *Pilgrim's Progress* – its first paragraph likens the father and son to 'pilgrims in a fable' – *The Road* recounts a progress that takes the unnamed principal characters on a gruelling journey of several months.[3] If this establishes the manner in which the novel is to be read, *The Road* can be thought of as symbolic or, better yet, as mimetic and allegorical. Allegories are rare among contemporary novels, and the analogies within them should not be pushed as hard as the interpreters of former ages pushed their sometimes fanciful allegorical readings of biblical narratives. Nor should readers assume that each element of this north-south, cross-country journey represents something specific in the way each element in Bunyan's fable does. At first glance, *The Road* may seem barren terrain to fuel discussion of religious and theological themes, but this barrenness deceives: the novel is a stark examination of morality when set loose from its moorings in religious belief and human civilisation. It poses questions such as, 'What is the basis of morality if there is no God?' and 'Where lies meaning in life if there is no ultimate purpose?'

The novel is ambiguous about the existence of God from beginning to end. The man's first words spoken aloud are about his son: 'If he is not the word of God God never spoke' (3). Later the boy is fondly described as a 'golden chalice, good to house a god' (78). But neither of these statements definitively express belief in God's existence; rather, they express the possibility that God is a possibility that is met by silence into which a god might speak, and by emptiness in which a god might be accommodated. When he wakes in the ashes after the catastrophic fire, the man calls out to God, 'Have you a neck by which to throttle you? Have you a heart? Damn you eternally have you a soul?' (10). He wonders whether he will see God at the last or, indeed, whether God is there at all. The philosopher of religion Erik Wielenberg is prepared to see the hand of God implicated in the frequent recurrence of almost-miraculous rescues of father and son from imminent demise in the novel.[4] I find no textual evidence for this implication, but the text does support the notion that a divine imperative drives the father. Although uncertain of God's existence, the man's conviction that he must face reality, that he must find ways to persevere, survive and thrive purposefully in

3. The link with Bunyan is made by Vanderheide, (2008), pp. 107-20.
4. Wielenberg, (2010), p. 1.

this post-apocalyptic world, gives a sense of divine mission about his peregrinations. His pilgrim's progress is a determined quest, despite knowing that his search may be futile, and he uses the idea that he is carrying fire to motivate himself and his son. Fire, which has been the means by which his familiar world has been destroyed, and the mastery of which is also the foundation of human civilisation, is their consolation on their journey: because they carry the fire, they believe nothing bad can happen to them (87). What then does this fire represent? Andrew Tate, in an article in *The Church Times*[5] saw distinctively Trinitarian language overarching the book, in that there is a strong bond between father and son while they carry the third person of the Trinity within them. The fire they carry is perhaps Pentecostal flame. On the other hand, it is possible to read the fire as merely a crude myth the man and his son fabricate to keep themselves on the road. Supporting the spiritual symbolism, and against the reduced symbolism, lies the insight that only the good guys carry fire, suggesting it may be a symbol of goodness.

Only two types of people populate the devastated world they walk through. Its tattered post-apocalyptic society is reduced to good guys and bad guys, distinguished by their readiness or otherwise to descend into cannibalism: bad guys eat people, good guys would rather go hungry. Wielenberg identifies six rules the good guys adopt as their moral code: do not eat people, do not steal, do not lie, keep promises, help others and never give up. These, however, are not absolute moral imperatives, they are not always easy to keep and sometimes circumstances compromise the wisdom of the rule. For instance, when they encounter a man who has been struck by lightning, the boy is keen to help, but his father argues against offering assistance because there is nothing they can do to save the man and, if they share their food and drink with him, they will imperil their own lives without any lasting benefit to him (53). Furthermore, the man promises never to leave his son, even in death. Consoling though this may be, it is a rash promise over which he has no ultimate control. Wielenberg calls this a 'slippery-slope problem'[6] that is part of humankind's struggle to be moral beings. Thus, McCarthy shows that morality is always more complex than a simple binary right and wrong or good and bad. Real life is more complicated than that.

Part of life's complexity concerns the discovery of meaning and purpose. This quest for meaning perhaps provides shape to the father and son's journey as they struggle to find purpose: how can life be meaningful in this dystopic world? In a flashback episode, the man

5. Tate, (2017), p. 22.
6. *op. cit.*, p. 7.

recalls a conversation he had had with his wife. To his suggestion that
they were survivors, she responded, 'What in God's name are you talking
about? We're not survivors. We're the walking dead in a horror film' (57).
Earlier the man and boy had been camped near a waterfall when the boy
had a dream about a toy penguin that woke him: 'I had this penguin that
you wound up and it would waddle and flap its flippers. And we were
in that house that we used to live in and it came around the corner but
nobody had wound it up and it was really scary. . . . The winder wasn't
turning' (37).

This inexplicable, pointless perpetual motion serves as an image for
the potentially meaningless existence that entraps man and boy. All
that prevents the man and boy from being walking dead or clockwork
penguins are the human relationships that develop on the journey, any
hospitality they show to the other and the development of friendships.

The man and boy have nine potentially dangerous encounters with
other humans on their journey south. These are the aforementioned
meeting with a man who was beyond help after being struck by lightning,
and a second with a roadrat, the word by which the bad guys on the road
are known. This roadrat discovers them accidentally when he goes into
the trees to relieve himself. This is a moment of real danger (65). A
third is with a group of scavengers marching along the road from whom
they hide themselves. Later they discover a group of prisoners held in
the basement of a plantation house for future slaughter as meat. Their
next encounter is with a half-blind old man, whom they feel confident
they can help because they realise there is little chance of his being a
decoy for an ambush (171). Their sixth encounter is with four people
including a pregnant woman who, when they are moved on, leave behind
'a charred human infant headless and gutted and blackening on the spit'
(212). They have been reduced to cannibalism. Later they meet a thief
who steals their shopping trolley full of goods (273), and a sniper who
ambushes them from the upper window of a house as they pass through
an otherwise abandoned town (281). The son's last encounter is after his
father's death, when he meets a shotgun-toting stranger and his family
who extend an open-armed welcome to the orphaned boy (301). The
risk entailed in some of these encounters is countermanded by offers
of cautious trust, but some have no chance of becoming exchanges of
hospitality and are therefore doomed to be themselves unproductive
of anything other than violence. If human beings, human society and
human culture depend on the exchange of hospitality for their survival,
The Road shows that the first step towards recovery and wellbeing is to
establish a mutual understanding that we each have responsibility to the

other, whether absent or with us. We see this most clearly in the father-son relationship, but we can see it, too, in the son's disappointment with his parent and the boy's ensuing silence when the man fails to act by their shared moral code. As the father says, 'The day [is] providential to itself' (56); each day provides opportunity to live morally, to forge human relations and to care for the Other.

One poignant moment in their journey is a brief conversation when the boy admits he had many friends, whom he remembers, and whom he misses because they had died in the catastrophe (61). At the end of the novel, once the boy is in the care of his new family, he draws comfort from remembering and trying to perpetuate the 'flawed but clearly real relationship he had had with his earthly father'.[7] In the book's final pages, the boy's foster mother often talks to him about God, but it is his earthly father, not God, he speaks to when he prays (306). Human connections have given him purpose for living in a bleak world. Thus, Wielenberg suggests that the novel demonstrates that belief in God is not as important as we take it to be.[8] Love is more valuable than all else, and the novel encourages belief in humanity as the basis on which any attempt to be one of the good guys becomes worthwhile. Phillip A. Snyder suggests that human cultures and society are dependent for their coherence upon hospitality, which he calls 'the condition of existence'.[9] If this is so, then we can read this pilgrimage novel as a narrative showing that human beings have an essential responsibility to the other, before self.

In 2014, Andrew Michael Hurley turned from publishing short stories and began a career writing novels that might be described as occult novels, for they deal with hidden aspects of life. They delve into themes of spiritual and supernatural experiences, often finding dark and extraordinary places in the ordinary and discovering more than meets the eye in the world around their characters. The first of these was *The Loney*, which like McCarthy's *The Road* recounted a pilgrimage. In this novel, the pilgrimage is an annual one taken by a Catholic family, not from a dystopic catastrophe to a probably better future, but from home life in London to a place where strange things happen, a 'strange nowhere', a stretch of land on the east coast of Lancashire known as the Loney. They lodge there in Moorings. It is a retreat centre where the family seeks healing for one of their two sons, Hanny, who is severely handicapped. Much about the place is eerie. The narrator finds much of the story he

7. *ibid.*, p. 12.
8. *ibid.*, p. 14.
9. Snyder, (2008), p. 85.

tells and much of its setting unsettling: there was often 'something [he] picked up with a different sense'. He never feels that this otherness was attributable to anything as ridiculous as ghosts and the like, but there was 'something nevertheless' (117). There had been a gap in their annual trips after the sudden departure of its usual leader, Father Wilfred. On the occasion of the first visit since this gap, the pilgrimage is led by Father Bernard who falls short of the high expectations established by his predecessor. The room the brothers share is at the top of the house where they find an old rifle under the floorboards and later Farther, the boys' father, reports finding a room, the door to which had been hidden behind a wall tapestry in the study. When he gains access to the room he finds it contains a bed and some toys. He thinks it might have been used to quarantine sick children, but is mystified that it is an adjunct of the study.

Around the time that Farther discovers this room, on a wet day when they are unable to go outside, the narrator, whom Father Bernard nicknames Tonto, recalls becoming a server back home at St Jude's Church. Its architecture looms over young children: an Eye of God on the steeple watched over them looking out for the seditious and the workshy, the pulpit was like a watchtower, and a life-sized crucified Christ was suspended before a vast window in such a way that its shadow fell over all the congregation. His induction as a server by Father Wilfred was far from kindly. The priest barks out questions like an army officer and indicates that any sloppiness in the conduct of their duties is a discourtesy to both him and God (101-7). Further evidence of Father Wilfred's cruelty emerges: he uses the edge of a metal ruler to strike the knuckles of a server who was late for Mass (129) and threatens him with the torment of hell as a liar because he does not believe the boy's excuse (132). After the same boy's mother reports that he was keeping 'vile magazines' in his bedroom, Father Wilfred asks him who will be cast down the deepest on the Day of Judgement. Father Wilfred supplies the answer to his own question – onanists, meaning boys who masturbate over such magazines – and forces the boy to grasp a handful of nettles, squeezing them until green juice ran down his arms. The episode ends sinisterly when Father Wilfred entreats the witnesses, 'Not a word, boys. These lessons are for you and nobody else' (166).

Father Bernard's dog, Monro, finds the carcase of a sheep in the woods. It was hanging from a tree and a twisted band of barbed wire had been hammered into its skull. Father Bernard and Farther entertained no doubts that this was meant to be an effigy of Christ, to offend the pilgrims. They notice there is something inside. When they investigate further, a pig's heart stuck through with nails falls to the ground (158).

In another remembered episode from the time of Father Wilfred, the narrator and his fellow-server, Henry, discuss whether or not to believe in hell, as Henry had been threatened with hell to such an extent that he is genuinely fearful. The narrator believes in it as much as he believes in Father Christmas. He is adamant that it is does not exist, and that it is no more than an idea that originated in people's imagination (209). On the other hand, is the Loney a form of hell?

On Easter Day, the Church is ransacked and the pilgrims are locked out. They persuade Father Bernard to say Mass outside the church, then return to Moorings to eat dinner. They cut the Simnel cake after throwing the ball of marzipan representing Judas onto the fire, and as they applaud the defeat of the betrayer they hear an ominous screech from outside. In the excitement, Monro knocks over a jar that was meant to keep evil spirits at bay. As it crashes to the floor, a stench fills the room and urine flows from the jar (222). The local resident, Clement, had regarded the jar as an effective deterrent to witches (228).

In the garden of healing at the Loney, Hanny is expected to drink holy water, but he is terrified. His mother, Esther, in her long-held desperation to find a cure for Hanny, forces him to drink by pinching his cheeks so that his mouth opens. She may have hurt him (263). Ultimately, Hanny is cured, but it takes Parkinson and Collier, two local sceptical ruffians suspected of some of the earlier sabotage, to bring the pilgrims to accept it:

> It's funny, int it? How you church people can have more faith in something that can't be proved than something that's standing right in front of you. I suppose it comes down to seeing what you want to see, dunt it? But sometimes you dunt get a choice. Sometimes the truth comes along whether that wants it to or not (297-8).

Yet Father Bernard's suggestion that 'there are only versions of the truth' (359) seems more in keeping with the author's purpose in making this novel. For this reason, I call this a novel of the occult: it uncovers the hidden and queries the absolute.

The haunting menace of *The Loney* continued in Hurley's next novel, *Devil's Day* (2017), where all that goes wrong and all that is unsettling is attributed to the devil. Here Hurley describes the devil's ubiquity:

> she'd come to understand what I meant when I said the Devil was real. Not the soppy Owd Feller in the songs, or the thing Gideon Denning and his friends thought they'd woken at Far

Lodge. There was nothing to wake anyway. The Devil has been here since before anyone came, passing endlessly from one thing to another. He's in the rain and the gales and the wild river. He's in the trees of the Wood. He's the unexpected fire and the biter of dogs. He's the disease that can ruin a howl farm and the blizzard that buries a whole village. But at least here we can see him at work (290-1).

Although hidden from sight, local people believe they see the effects of the devil's work:

The lambs that had grown strong and weighty on mosscrop over the summer began to die for no reason. The dogs went blind and their eyes teemed with white worms. The mushrooms that the farming families always collected from the Wood in autumn now brought on seizures and the Gaffer's newly-wed sister, Emily, who had laughed the loudest when her father had spilled his port-wine, fell down in convulsions and swallowed her tongue (66).

The young priest who comes to read the last rites over her body has rational explanations for all these events:

it was easy enough to see what had happened. The lambs had simply picked up some disease from the moors and passed it on to the dogs. And the mushrooms, well, these people had obviously mistaken one species for another . . . and fired up a pan of toxic gills and stalks by accident (67).

Despite his more rational turn of mind, the priest humours the family in their superstitious talk of the devil. Belief in the real presence of the devil goes almost unquestioned among local people in the Endlands, where the novel is set, yet only Laurel, who arranges the Gaffer's funeral, has any interest in religion. Some local people had gone to the local Catholic school, but that was only because it was by far the closest school and the custom of giving people a Christian burial was 'just a necessary bit of theatre that meant the dear departed could stay in the valley' (41). Although religious observance has all but disappeared among the people of the Endlands, having waned as much as it has waned in contemporary British society, folk-memory retains a potent mythology giving supernatural explanations for misfortune. Similarly, in early twenty-first-century societies where people have become less religiously observant, remnants of orthodox religious beliefs continue to inform conversations and practices, especially around death. Often these have been debased, corrupted or sentimentalised. These include the piles of floral tributes laid at the scenes of sudden deaths and the increased interest in aspects of angelology such as guardian angels. Some of this results from the failure of organised religion to engage successfully with people at times of bereavement, and some is simply to do with loss of orthodox belief wrestling with the innate spirituality people have as naturally religious beings. Secular folk theology such as this is not entirely divorced from the Christian tradition, and we should perhaps find ways to use it to speak theologically to today's world.

Hurley's portrait of the devil is problematic for many contemporary Christians, for it can be dangerous to retain belief in personified malevolence while ditching other mythological aspects of Christianity. Folk-memory, while having many positive elements, can compromise or hinder the claims of orthodox faith, so the modern Church must be careful when it draws on secular folk theology in its apologetics and evangelism.

Brian Catling, a poet and sculptor who publishes fantasy fiction as B. Catling, began a trilogy in 2007 with *The Vorrh*. A second edition was issued in 2012. The Vorrh of the title is a primaeval semi-tropical forest in the heart of Africa, unmapped and immeasurable. It may or may not be the location of the Garden of Eden, and near it, some believe, roam Adam, Eve and their children, now reduced to degenerate cannibals. As the outbreak of the Second World War looms, the region is inhabited by monsters and exploited by colonialists. One aspect of the fantasy of the novel is that the region of the Vorrh is itself a sentient being who permits a small number of individuals to hack a wedge in it at its southern edge to take timber. Trade in this timber has created on the outskirts of the Vorrh a large but decaying, European-style city, Essenwald, where mansions display the original inhabitants' wealth, and from which a train makes regular journeys taking tourists, explorers and slave-worker lumberjacks in and out of the forest.

Catling's work contributes to a sub-genre within fantasy fiction sometimes called 'the new weird'.[10] The weirdness is heralded in the opening scene of the novel where a man carves himself a sentient bow from the spine of his deceased lover. Weirdness never leaves the book: a boy in Essenwald is educated by one-eyed Bakelite robots in underground rooms watched over by a mysterious and punitive observer,

10. See Kelly, (2017), p. 9.

and this observer punishes another under observation by taking his son away and returning him with his hands sewn on backwards. This weirdness demonstrates the moral and physical corruption of the tainted and addicted population of *The Vorrh*.

Despite this weirdness, the novel has a classic quest structure in that its overarching narrative tells of the Bowman, armed with a massive pistol as well as his sentient bow and arrows, aiming to cross the Vorrh. Meanwhile a human native, Tsungali, pursues the Bowman with the intention of killing him with the Lee Enfield rifle issued to Tsungali when he had served as a colonial police officer. The Bowman's quest and the pursuer's chase frame the fantasy.

The Vorrh is a long novel and specific references to Christian theology and religion are few. However, its very core and basis is the Eden myth, from which Catling raises several concomitant theological and spiritual themes for the Christian reader: not only Eden and paradise, but also the source of religion, the concept of the sacred, the nature of redemption and the instinct to pray.

Catling recounts the origin of religion in the Vorrh and its environs:

> the strangers settled in and brought families and new beliefs to the village. . . . They instructed the True People in the way of the one world, with its god ashamed of nakedness. They taught them how work might bring them those precious things that were previously given. They brought books and singing and exchanged the splendour of an invisible god for all their carved deities of wood and stone. And somewhere in that sickly trade, suspicion became woven into the fabric of trust. The insistence of guilt was converted into the notion that the True People must have already paid the price for something, something they had never received, something that might just be possessions (22-3).

What is this but a satire on European colonialism in Africa, when native Africans were clothed in Western attire in response to hearing the gospel of salvation?

An early citation of lines from Book V of Milton's *Paradise Lost*, accompanied by a description of an illustration from an edition of the poem found by a priest, establishes the fantasy's intertextuality with the Eden myth. Soon readers learn that Eden is located in the Vorrh, where 'God walks, to think in worldly ways'. In Eden, which is located on Earth, not remote in a distant prelapsarian and inaccessible past, God 'wears a gown of senses, woven in our time . . . [and] pictures our life in the matter that makes us' (66). In the Vorrh, Adam's fate is not that of the biblical Adam who died. In the Vorrh, 'the truth is told. Adam was never completely forgiven; his sons and daughters left this place and occupied the world. He waited for God, waited for forgiveness and for his rib to grow back. But he became tired of waiting, and walked back into the forest.' Now Adam is forgotten, 'each century he loses a skin of humanity, peeling back through the animals to dust' (220-1). What does this suggest about the nature of humanity? Is it a reversal of the notion that humankind is on an upward spiral? And is it an expression of our inevitable integration with both the animal kingdom and the earth, and humanity's inevitable humiliation reduced to the dust from which we came?

Christians find it difficult to discuss Eden without thinking of redemption. In the Vorrh there exists a pilgrim's chapel to provide shelter and refuge for those who travel near the Vorrh's sacred heart. Tucked away in a dark corner of the chapel hangs a painting whose coat of varnish had turned so black that the picture seemed either empty or a dark portrait of 'painted night'. The story behind the picture is that it is of a 'Black Faced Man' who protects the tree in Eden after all the sons of Adam are dead (76-7). This gives the traveller a taste of redemption and a sense that salvation might 'shudder' in some of the 'ludicrous myths of the Vorrh' that 'talked of the serpent sin, of deliverance, of the starry crown, and the origin of purpose' (76). Catling is doing no more here than merely hinting at a pressing dilemma for humanity that struggles to find a way back to proximity with divinity, but the hint is sufficient to set readers thinking. How can redemption be found? How is salvation bestowed? Where can we find our way back – or is it a way forward – to be with God?

Linking all of this is the concept of the Vorrh as a sacred and forbidden place. Travellers are told they can visit the heart of the Vorrh a maximum of three times in their lives. The Vorrh, as a taboo place, a holy place, 'is sacred, from its outer rings to its core' (183). Intrusion into its time and its space, except for the segment where timber cutting is permitted, will offend. In the forest, where foreboding and dread readily set in, the traveller finds himself tempted to prayer. But that natural human instinct to pray is squashed by the rational mind:

> A prayer almost found its way to his lips. It began in the
> icy fear of his heart, the ventricles white with the frost of
> anticipation, and travelled outwards to become a pressure, like

the wind against the meat sails of his lungs. Funnelling up, it passed like a shadow through the rehearsal of his vocal cords, up into his mouth, tongue and lips, before being garrotted by the thin, taut wire of his mind (217).

I find it interesting, even ironic, that in this instance fantasy fiction chooses to give priority to the rational mind's tendency to suppress the traveller's natural instinct to take recourse to prayer when he is filled with fear of the unknown.

For the remainder of this chapter we turn to a novel telling a story that claims to make you believe in God, Yann Martel's *Life of Pi* (2002). The most popular Booker Prize winner in terms of sales, *Life of Pi* is an ascent, or a quest, narrative – a journey towards enlightenment – told by Piscine Molitor Patel (Pi), who survives 277 days adrift in the Pacific Ocean after the Japanese ship carrying his family and its zoo collection from Pondicherry to Canada sinks. Initially marooned on a lifeboat with a hyena, a zebra with a broken leg, an orangutan and an adult male Bengal tiger, for most of the time he is alone with the tiger until the boat washes up on the coast of Mexico. There Pi stumbles ashore and the tiger disappears into the jungle. When Japanese Ministry of Transport accident investigators doubt his account, he supplies an alternative, perhaps more credible, version of his survival story in which he replaces the animals with people. Pi then asks the investigators which story they prefer: 'Which is the better story, the story with animals or the story without animals?' When both officials, somewhat surprisingly given their scepticism, choose the story with animals, Pi replies, 'Thank you. And so it goes with God' (317). It seems a story with God in it is preferable to, or better than, a story without God, yet few critics and readers have been convinced. High praise has been expressed for the novel and Martel's narrative skills, but few have been 'made to believe in God' as the author's note promises. This author's note is a conceit, of course. It is the pretext for the novel: when the novel's author-narrator meets Francis Adirubasamy in a coffee house in Pondicherry, Adirubasamy gives him the novel's tale and Adirubasamy promises him it will make him believe in God. As a discourse on the nature of belief, *Life of Pi* raises at least three significant religious themes.

The first concerns our view of humanity. The close proximity to animals that Pi experiences throughout his precarious voyage allows Martel to discuss humanity's distinctive features. Like Robinson Crusoe, to whom Pi as a lone survivor against the odds has been compared, Pi survives through the application of calculated rationality: Martel says that reason is the very best toolkit (298). Pi's rationality begins, as Crusoe's had done, with his taking of an inventory of everything he salvages from the shipwreck. Like Crusoe, he sets about establishing his dominance over nature by establishing a type of farm: Crusoe grew vegetables on his farm while Pi's crop is fresh water from solar stills. The dominance he most pressingly needs to assert, however, is over Richard Parker, the Bengal tiger. He controls the tiger first by giving it a man's name, then by rocking the boat and prodding it with a stick after intentionally tempting it to invade his personal space. His rationale is that, because animals are territorial and prone to seasickness, the tiger will associate venturing into Pi's section of the boat with nausea and choose to stay away. The critic, Philip Armstrong, who makes this comparison with Crusoe, comments that 'Pi dominates the tiger, and therefore survives, because humans are good travellers and animals are not.'[11]

Whether or not animals are essentially territorial, the point is that the novel suggests that what distinguishes humanity from animals is that we rove the planet. Martel, who has lived in at least six countries, regards global mobility as fundamental to human nature.[12] We move, we travel and we explore to discover exciting unfamiliar experiences, while animals restrict themselves to a certain territory for their hunting and foraging. Nonetheless, the wild tiger was trapped in a zoo, given an English name, shipped across the world on a container ship and trained like a circus animal before, in the end, running off into the jungle where it belonged, free and no longer under human bondage.

Martel's depiction of the animals in *Life of Pi* verges on anthropomorphism, which we would usually regard as inappropriate because it attributes to animals human characteristics that undervalue their 'animalness'. Indeed, Pi's father had taught him that the most dangerous animal in Pondicherry zoo is *'animalus anthropomorphicus'* because when we see animals through human eyes, we put ourselves at the centre and that, he says, 'is the bane not only of theologians but also of zoologists' (31). Yet I suggest there may be border territory that is safe to tread: David Attenborough would not anthropomorphise, but those who keep pets know that their animals have feelings – they can be happy and sad, sulking and cooperative – and, as companions, they become almost as valuable as humans.

All this begs a question that takes us on a short anthropological and theological detour: what distinguishes humans from animals? Something must, for we call subhuman or inhumane behaviour bestial. That's not

11. Armstrong, (2008), p. 178.
12. *ibid.*, p. 179.

to say, however, that animal behaviour is intentionally cruel. It just is as it is. I heard a discussion on a recent radio programme in which some researchers observing chimpanzees – our near relatives – noted that chimpanzee parents are more protective of their children than human parents are of theirs. Human parents pass their babies around, with different mothers prepared to look after different babies and willing to show them off to friends and family. Chimpanzees are more protective of their babies because adult chimpanzees eat young chimpanzees. They also noted that chimpanzee parents feed themselves before feeding their young. Among human adults and in human families, guests and children are given priority. If you come to dine in my home I am unlikely to keep the best food for myself, but I might if I am being less than human. Apes eat the best food for themselves and give the stalks to their children because the animal instinct is for self-preservation.

Perhaps the fundamental difference is that humans are sentient beings. We think, we emote, we feel, we reason, we understand what we do, we can choose to change our behaviour. Sentience provides humans with a sense of religiosity; we can think ourselves into religious stances; we can imagine God or 'no God', theism or atheism.

This takes us to the second religious theme of the novel. It offers an interesting treatise on the plurality of religious faiths. In his early life, Pi had been inspired by a charismatic biology teacher, Mr Kumar, who, as an active communist declared he had no belief in religion. Now, Pi conversely collects religions as if they are souvenirs gathered on his lifelong voyage of self-discovery. Mr Kumar described religion as darkness and tells Pi how, as a child, he lay in bed asking, 'Where is God?', and because God never came, reason became his prophet. This, said Pi, 'was [his] first clue that atheists are [his] brothers and sisters of a different faith, and every word they speak speaks faith' (28). Before the mature Pi reaches that conclusion, the youthful Pi picks up Hinduism, Christianity and Islam. Beginning with the notion that we are all born, like Catholics he says, into limbo without religion until someone introduces us to God, Pi's introduction to God was through his aunt who took him to a Hindu temple when he was still a small baby. On that day, 'a germ of religious exaltation, no bigger than a mustard seed, was sown in me and left to germinate. It has never stopped growing' (47). For the remainder of chapter 16 he explains why he is a Hindu. His next religious excursion is an encounter with Christianity in the form of a Catholic priest whom he meets regularly over the course of three days spent in Munnar. He regards Christianity as a religion with 'one Story' (53). Pi contrasts these two religions:

> Christianity is a religion in a rush. . . . If Hinduism flows placidly like the Ganges, then Christianity bustles like Toronto in the rush hour. It is a religion as swift as a swallow, as urgent as an ambulance. It turns on a dime, expresses itself in the instant. In a moment you are lost or saved (57).

He thanks Lord Krishna for having put Jesus of Nazareth where Pi might meet him. 'Islam followed right behind, hardly a year later' (58). A Sufi mystic teaches him to seek union with God and he enjoys the presence of God as the reward of his spiritual peregrinations, describing himself as 'a practising Hindu, Christian and Muslim' (64) whose house is filled with Hindu gods, a framed photograph of the Kaaba in Mecca and several images of the Virgin Mary. He regularly invokes 'Jesus, Mary, Mohammed and Vishnu', 'God' or 'Allah', but, in the second part of the novel while he is on the lifeboat, no Jonah-like anguished questioning troubles his faith. Although his parents and some of their religious confidants had tried to make him choose one faith from the several he likes, he adamantly lives by the creed he learnt from Gandhi: all religions are true (69). When espousing a religion, all that humans are trying to do is trying to love God.

Of course, this claim raises an important question about the genuineness of religious faith and the various models of interfaith connectedness. Traditionally the relationship between Christianity and other religions has been described as either exclusive, inclusive or pluralist. The first maintains that there is no salvation for people outside Christianity; the second, an inclusive model, maintains that God may save those of other faiths; and the pluralist model assumes that all faiths lead to God. None of these models are problem-free. The exclusive model seems to limit the scope of God's love, the inclusive model implies that non-Christian faiths can be intentional revelations of God, and not all Christian believers are comfortable with that, and the pluralist model denies the uniqueness or specialness of any faith, which might trouble followers of any religion. Currently, after several decades of inter-faith dialogue, the state of theological scholarship is such that the inadequacy of the traditional models and the need for something of a paradigm shift are recognised, so that we can have theologies that find common ground, share common statements and yet embrace difference.[13]

The third aspect of Martel's novelistic treatment of the nature of belief lies in the phenomenon of story, a recurring theme in the novels we are discussing in *Make-Believe*, and this takes us back to the question posed

13. See Kibble, (2019).

at the conclusion of Pi's storytelling: which do you prefer, the one with animals or the one without, the one with magic or the one without, the one with God or the one without? In a published interview with Andrew Steinmetz, Martel linked story and religion by alluding to Coleridge's 'suspension of disbelief'.[14] He said that religion operates in the exact same way a novel operates: a good novel works when you suspend your disbelief and a good religion also makes you suspend disbelief. This troubles the critic James Wood, for it appears to conflate belief in a story with belief in God.[15] The problem, I think, is the basis on which hearers choose which story they prefer. Do they prefer the story with the animals because it is true or because it is more aesthetically pleasing and entertaining? Similarly, do we prefer the story with God in it because it is true or more pleasing to the ear? For at least one literary critic, Stewart Cole, this matters because, like the tiger who ran irretrievably into the jungle on reaching dry land in Mexico, he fears God will disappear when the story with God in it stops being told.[16] For many religious believers, story is paramount. We live by a Story, whose historicity is unimportant, for what matters is the narratival and theological truth it carries. Telling and retelling the story, not because it is an historical account, but because it in some way explains the human experience and predicament becomes the purpose of communities of faith.

Martel likened religion to zoos. Both, he says, face the same problem of 'illusions about freedom' (19) in that both are regarded as places where freedom is restricted: freedom of movement is lacking in zoos and freedom of thought is often missing in religion. Perhaps, though, *Life of Pi*'s story is not so much a story to make us believe in God as a narrative of self-discovery. If this is so, *Life of Pi* truly offers, as Philip Armstrong says, a rhapsody to the power of the human spirit.[17]

Fantasy fiction hymns the power of humanity. While much fantasy fiction makes space for religious ritual and catches glimpses into the realm of the supernatural and spiritual, thereby making space for God, most fantasy fiction lauds the wonder of humanity in our ability to imagine utopias and to survive dystopias. Some would nonetheless call that ability God-given.

---

14. Reported in Cole, (2004), p. 23.
15. *op. cit.*, p. 23.
16. *op. cit.*, p. 35.
17. *op. cit.*, p. 179.

Chapter 5

HISTORICAL NOVELS
'The present . . . throwing its shadow backwards?'[1]

The 2018 Reith Lectures, broadcast as usual on BBC Radio 4, gave one of the best-known living historical novelists, Hilary Mantel, an opportunity to reflect in public on the intricacies of her craft. Among the invited guests attending the second lecture in London were two actors who had played her character Thomas Cromwell: one on stage, Ben Miles, the other in the television series, Mark Rylance. The host, Sue Lawley, asked each whether Cromwell was a religious man. Although they saw differing aspects of religion in the character they played, both affirmed that religion drove him.

Religion – in the form of religious observance, faith, folklore and superstition – has a special role in historical fiction, where, even when it is not the driving force as it was in Mantel's *Wolf Hall*, it is often deployed to help establish the temporal setting for the action. Historical fiction is a popular and broad genre resisting precise classification, though the Walter Scott Prize for Historical Fiction sets at least one boundary: to qualify for the award, historical novels must be set at least sixty years before the publication date. Often religion, or a character's expression of belief, helps to establish the novel's historical context.

A natural affinity exists between history and fiction, intimated in the linguistic coincidence that, in several European languages, the same word means both story and history. For example, in French *histoire* means both. This affinity blurs a customary distinction between the modern historian, who aspires towards the unattainable ideal of objectivity, and the contemporary historical novelist, whose business is to reconstruct the past in fictional form. As the twentieth century drew to a close, the literary critic David Price observed that history is not an univocal what-really-happened, but a polyvocal competition of discourse, languages and points of view.[2]

---

1. Margaret Drabble cited in Higdon, (1984), p. 134.
2. Price, (1999), p. 9.

Robert Holton had previously called these 'jarring witnesses'.[3] Another important distinction is that between the past and history: in conversation I often find myself using the term history as a synonym for the past, but this is misleading. The past is not history. History is one way of telling the past, a method we use to organise the past. Historical fiction is an alternative method. Price noted that history is made, not found: archaeologists, for instance, find artefacts, not history, and these objects help them to weave a narrative that makes a history. We might therefore regard the past as a fictive realm, the composite of stories woven around found records and things.

In his discussion of historical novels, David Higdon suggested that novels explore the past in three main ways. First, in some novels, characters confront their own pasts. This is likely to occur in any novel genre where the formation of character and the motivation of a character are common preoccupations of novelists. Second, some fiction self-consciously imitates or rewrites earlier fiction. Recently, several publishing houses have purposefully encouraged rewrites by commissioning novelistic retellings of Shakespeare plays and Greek tragedies. Thus, the ancient texts enjoy afterlives. In the third group, the past is chosen as the setting for novels as a way of playing with the content and values of the present. In such cases, the novel, set in an age we have not lived in, holds a mirror up to the present age and contemporary readers, and gives us a protected environment where we can safely recognise something familiar and comfortably explore the immediacy of our own surroundings. In this sense historical fiction is akin to science fiction: both use estrangement to make connections. In the case of historical novels, novelists take readers in their imaginations into a form of the past where they can recognise both themselves and the current age in which they live.

Conventionally, Sir Walter Scott's *Waverley* (1814) is usually regarded as the first historical novel. Scott supplied an author's note, thereby unconsciously establishing a precedent for many future historical novels. Many historical novelists have since felt they needed to supply extratextual information in the form of a note that distances the novelist from the history; this indicates that fiction always distorts fact yet claims some level of authenticity. Jerome de Groot sees the prevalence of such authorial notes as an indication that the writers are aware that writing historical fiction is a strange exercise in which the boundaries between fiction and fact begin to blur.[4] Other critics have suggested the genre is more like 'faction'. Historical novels do not misrepresent the past, but

3. Holton, (1994), *passim*.
4. De Groot, (2010), p. 9.

they tell it in ways other than an historian would. The novelist takes the bare bones of the past and tells stories within the gaps. In 1924, the historian Herbert Butterfield wrote a treatise on historical novels, mainly those by Sir Walter Scott, in which he described them as a fusion, a form of history and a way of treating the past.[5] His knowledge and expertise as an historian taught him that history was full of tales half-told, and of songs broken off midstream that yearn to be filled out, and of which we long for a fuller vision.[6] As an historian, Butterfield argued that historical fiction can provide that fuller vision by enabling what he called imaginative understanding.

The breadth of the genre of historical fiction is evidenced in de Groot's list of types. First, romances for women, usually written by women for a predominantly female audience, do not meet universal approval as they tend to be conservative and perpetuate the hegemony of patriarchy. One of the key strands of the publishing house Mills and Boon, whose sales number hundreds of millions worldwide, is an historical romance series whose presence within the genre of historical fiction should not be overlooked. Georgette Heyer, Catherine Cookson and Barbara Cartland are the biggest selling among a long list of writers of such romances. Related to these are adventures for men, just as formulaic and conservative as romances for women. C.S. Forester's Hornblower novels, Bernard Cornwell's Sharpe novels and Patrick O'Brian's Aubrey-Maturin seafaring tales often include much historical detail of military and naval tactics alongside the derring-do. The third group of historical novels are written to educate children. The Roman novels of Rosemary Sutcliff, who was motivated by an expressed desire to teach through fiction, are perhaps the best known. Many literary critics find the fourth category of historical fiction particularly intriguing. This is historiographic metafiction, an off-putting technical term that describes novels, such as John Fowles's *The French Lieutenant's Woman* (1969), A.S. Byatt's *Possession* (1990) and Rose Tremain's *Restoration* (1989), that self-consciously play with their presentation of the past. In historiographic metafiction, the writer never lets the reader forget that the novel is a self-conscious fabrication. War novels constitute possibly the most popular form of historical fiction. Analysis of all 650 novels submitted during the eight years the Walter Scott Prize has functioned has revealed that four out of every ten were set in the twentieth century. The Second World War was the setting of fourteen per cent of all submissions, and the First World War nine per cent. These seem small

5. Butterfield, (1924), pp. 3 and 6.
6. *ibid.*, pp. 15-16.

percentages, but given the scope of human history novelists could draw on, the concentrated focus on two wars within the last 100 years or so is significant. Perhaps Pat Barker's *Regeneration* trilogy (1991-2005), Ian McEwan's *Atonement* (2002) and Sebastian Barry's *A Long, Long Way* (2005) demonstrate above all else that, because wartime is taxing, the bleakness and violence of war pushes the human condition to its limits. Consequently, these periods give novelists scope they cannot find in other eras.

De Groot's next four categories of historical fiction have in common the fact that they uncover alternative histories. These are counter-histories, forgotten histories, challenging histories and histories from the margins. These challenge normative readings of history by telling the past from overlooked perspectives so that marginalised people emerge as legitimate historical subjects and narrators. Such people include black, gay and lesbian people, as well as members of subjugated populations of nations previously governed by oppressive or imperialist regimes. Sarah Waters's *Tipping the Velvet* (2002) and *Fingersmith* (2003), Sebastian Barry's Irishman fighting for 'the English' in the First World War in *A Long, Long Way* (2005) and Peter Carey's depiction of Ned Kelly are among the examples de Groot notes, to which I add Andrea Levy's *Small Island* (2004) that gives the Windrush generation a voice.

The next group of historical fiction is a form of hybrid of two popular novel genres – historical and detective fiction. In historical detective stories, many of the investigators are monks (Ellis Peters's Cadfael and Umberto Eco's William of Baskerville), lawyers such as C.J. Sansom's Shardlake, and, of course, police officers. In these, the crime has often been committed in institutions and communities such as monasteries. This subgenre, because of its particular religious dimension, deserves separate attention in the next chapter.

The final group in de Groot's classification is genre-bending and postmodern. These are the counterfactual histories of 'What if?' These novels, telling a narrative as if something other than what actually happened has happened, have been dismissed as being as insubstantial as a literary parlour game, but they are more than that: their positing of an alternative reality can enable the exploration of assumptive attitudes. What if the Spanish Armada had been successful? What if Germany had won the Second World War? What if Stalin had had children? All these 'what ifs' have sparked counterfactual historical fictions in the last thirty years, each of which has challenged common assumptions and accepted norms.

The Problem and the Promise of Historical Fiction

One of the most influential of critics of historical fiction was György Lukács whose essay on the genre was published in 1955, again focused on Scott's novels. Three important insights come from the essay. First, as a Marxist literary theorist, Lukács discussed the Hegelian theory of process in history and asserted that history is constantly in a state of flux. None of us can escape being part of the forces of history that reach into and influence all human life. In short, all human life is steeped in history and its processes. Second, noting the historical faithfulness and accuracy of Scott as a writer, he observed that what mattered in historical fiction is not the retelling of historical events, but the establishment of a live connection between the there-and-then and the here-and-now so that through empathy 'we re-experience [the historical characters'] social and human motives'.[7] This achieves what Butterfield had previously called 'imaginative understanding'. Third, Lukács noted that Scott used 'necessary anachronism'. Anachronism, such as the reference to a mechanical clock in Act II of Shakespeare's *Julius Caesar*, is ordinarily either the result of a writer's oversight or inserted as a source of humour. However, Lukács's necessary anachronism 'consists simply in allowing . . . characters to express feelings and thoughts about real, historical relationships in a much clearer way than actual men and women of the time could have done'.[8] The characters have the benefit of some of the hindsight available to their authors. Each of these observations is to do with the essential connections between past and present, between writer and reader, and between historical character and actual historical figure. To achieve any of this, all historical novelists sculpt reality, forge history (using the term 'forge' in its non-pejorative sense, like a blacksmith) and make things up. They, too, are engaged in the art of manufacture and the game of make-believe.

The above concepts – the flux of history, living empathy and necessary anachronism – are essential to make historical fiction work, yet there are also other factors to bear in mind when discussing historical novels. The first is the interplay of defamiliarisation. When, in my doctoral studies, I considered the form and function of preaching in Geraldine Brooks's *Year of Wonders* and Jane Rogers's *Mr Wroe's Virgins*, I simplistically assumed that setting novels in the past is a defamiliarising technique that enables novelists to explore the immediacy of our surroundings in a non-threatening manner. Subsequent research and thought have moved

7. Cited in de Groot, (2010), p. 27.
8. Cited in de Groot, (2010), p. 28.

me towards a more nuanced opinion: modern parallels are not the primary business of the historical novelist. 'The past is not a rehearsal: it is the show itself,' said Hilary Mantel in her second Reith Lecture. However, reading the past may be like holding a mirror – it is where we can see ourselves – but both historians and historical novelists are equally irritated when commentators draw inadequate or inappropriate parallels. For instance, at the close of the second 2018 Reith Lecture, Diarmaid MacCulloch and Hilary Mantel shared their irritation at the comparison commonly made between the Reformation and Britain's planned exit from the European Union.

At the Hey Literary Festival in 2017, John Guy, a Tudor historian, was troubled that some hopeful students applying to read Tudor history at Cambridge seem to blur fact and fiction and have read nothing about Thomas Cromwell other than *Wolf Hall*, but he nonetheless supported the role of historical fiction. He remarked that historical novelists tell lies in order to tell the truth. Commenting on Hilary Mantel's work, he argued that she summons up ghosts, writes remarkably convincing dialogue and relies on the authority of imagination for legitimacy. This does not make her an inferior form of historian, he said, and it does not matter if factual inaccuracies occur in fiction. The trades, he said, are different but complementary.

History's accounts of the past are never innocent, despite the goal of objectivity. Each interpreter of the past brings preunderstanding to his or her research and some ideology may inform their analysis. As a result, all history is value-laden. Nevertheless, with careful scrutiny, such history can improve our understanding of the present and contribute to the creation of possible futures. This reminds me of a scene in Anne Michaels's *Fugitive Pieces* (1997). In the years after a Greek archaeologist called Athos rescues a Jewish boy from Auschwitz, he insists that the boy learns Hebrew. Why? Because, he said, he is thus remembering his future.[9]

One of the risks facing novelists writing of religion in former times is to fall into the assumptions of what Butterfield called the Whig interpretation of history. This is the notion that human history is on an inevitable and irrevocable course of improvement. In other words, people of a later age are always seen to be more sophisticated and intelligent than their predecessors. This complacent view of history as steady progress can tempt novelists into depicting religious believers of earlier ages as gullible and credulous. Their characters can slip into being simpler folk living in less complex times than ours, and this is an unfair representation of the role

9. Michaels, (1997), p. 21.

of faith in the past. Faith instilled the spirit of many past ages and drove many events and many people. The novelist Barry Unsworth distrusted historical minutiae and argued that what was essential was that novelists got hold of 'the spirit of the age, what it was like to be alive in that age, what it felt like to be an ordinary person in the margins of history'.[10] For Unsworth, this was more important than detail. This 'steeped-in sense of the religiosity of the past' is exactly what Suzi Feay, beginning her review of Beth Underdown's *The Witchfinder's Sister* in *The Guardian*, said novelists can find difficult to convey. This chapter shows that this religiosity is often a blend of orthodoxy, biblical literality and either folk religion or superstition. Even so, faith has been the driver of so much human conduct that Hilary Mantel, in the question-and-answer session at the end of her first Reith Lecture, commented that any novelist – whether or not writing novels set in the past – who chooses to step back from this truth and ignore religion, spirituality or theology is impoverished. Having been brought up Catholic, Mantel is thankful that she can therefore understand her characters. How well can readers without similar religious education or religious experience continue to understand the religion that drives so much of our literature? This troubling question and a related question – why do novelists include so much religious, theological and spiritual content in their books when British society, at least, is regarded as being less observant of religion? – lie at the heart of this book.

As I have drawn on so much of her theorising in what I have written above, you may think it is perverse that the case studies in this chapter will not include any of Mantel's novels. However, they are already widely discussed elsewhere, so I will instead draw attention to four recent, well-received novels: Ian Mortimer's *The Outcasts of Time* (2017), Sarah Perry's *The Essex Serpent* (2016), Geraldine Brooks's *People of the Book* (2008) and Beth Underdown's *The Witchfinder's Sister* (2017), two of which are remarkable debut novels.

Ian Mortimer's *The Outcasts of Time* ranges through several eras. The conceit at its heart is that the main characters make a pact by which they choose to travel through time at ninety-nine-year intervals for a day at a time. John of Wrayment is a stonemason who works on Exeter Cathedral in 1348. He and his brother, William Beard, who has a more devil-may-care attitude to life, experience a vision soon after John's wife, Catherine, succumbs to the plague. Visiting the cathedral where he had incorporated likenesses of his family in carvings, John hears a voice purporting to be his own voice. He calls it his conscience. I suspect

10. Cited by Clare Clark in her review of Helen Dunmore's *Birdcage Walk* in *The Guardian* (2017).

this is an instance of necessary anachronism, for I am not sure that a stonemason of that era would have naturally identified an inner voice as conscience. Indeed, later in the novel the source of the voice is a matter for debate. Was it God who addressed the brothers? Or the devil? The voice, also heard by William, informs John he has only six days to live and save his soul. He can either go home to die or do what no man has ever done before. As all around them people die of the plague, William and John begin to show the tell-tale symptoms that they have now contracted the disease, so they decide to choose the latter option and follow the instructions of the voice to go to the stone circle of Scorhill. There they will make their pact and choose to 'live their last six days in the distance of the future' (69).

I am reminded of Dr Who, *Groundhog Day* and H.G. Wells's *The Time Machine* as I read *The Outcasts of Time*. At the end of each day William and John go to sleep knowing that the next day they will wake up ninety-nine years later to live through 17 December yet again. Of course, because of the switch from the Julian to the Gregorian calendar, in 1843 and 1942 they find they live through 29 December. Mortimer, who is the author of a series of Time Travellers' Guides that give readers an idea of what it would be like to visit Medieval, Tudor and Restoration England, adapted and developed his successful format in fictional form in *The Outcasts of Time*. His characters, William and John, whizz through the centuries in less than a week, getting a quick taste of life in 1447, 1546, 1645, 1744, 1843 and 1942. John alone experiences the last three centuries, because, unbeknownst to him, William's pact had only been for three days.

The quaintness of their speech, the outdatedness of their clothes, their unfamiliarity with new inventions such as 'eye windows', clocks and 'chariots that move at the most incredible speeds without a single draught animal' (337), and the transmission of William's surname from 'of Wrayment' to Drayman, Offremont and Everyman, are not the only markers of their travel through the centuries. The changing shape of Christianity in Britain marks the passage of time, too, with the cathedral as its emblem.

In 1447, the town is served by a Canon Precentor from the cathedral who is also rector of the church, a resident vicar and a clerk of the chapel of St Margaret. On their quest to save their souls, William asks what a man must do to secure safe passage to heaven. Their host tells them that Rome teaches that they can clear out their souls of the taint of sin by purchasing indulgences, but their host is less certain. He recommends a pilgrimage to Jerusalem where they can wash their sins away through repentance at the Holy Sepulchre.

In 1546, they find themselves in danger as their Catholicism is the 'old religion'. The potential conflict between science and faith is anticipated as William and John puzzle over new-fangled clocks. They ask how clocks can tell time when time is reckoned by the motion of the sun around the Earth that is subject to the will of God. They become subject to hardship and the stonemason is reduced to smashing stones. William and John hear of gruesome persecutions such as that of Anne Askew, whose limbs were pulled from her body on the rack, for refusing to accept that any man could tell her the true meaning of what she could read for herself in the Bible. While witnessing the growth of Protestantism, John also notes the loss of something he had valued in his own faith: the sense of society and community in church. He remarks, 'We were far more united and accepting of God's will. In this new century, people are all divided and unsatisfied, hoping that God will smile on them personally' (152). I think this is an important observation: for twenty-first-century Christians, especially Protestant Christians, faith is often individualised, and there is less emphasis on the togetherness of community. This can be most evident at Holy Communion where the emphasis can be more on the believer's own one-to-one communion with Christ than on the communal nature of the meal as a foretaste of a heavenly banquet for all people.

John debates the Reformers' distrust of imagery with a traveller by the name of Richard Townsend. While John, as a Catholic, argues that sculptures evoke pure worship of God because they need no words, Richard points out that, soon after the monks were ordered out of the cathedral with an hour's notice and ordered to hand over all their gilt, silver and precious reliquaries, people learnt that all ornamentation in the cathedral, including the stonework John had worked on, was to go (145).

John and William awake in 1645 to the clamour of the Civil War, in which it is said that God's will will be expressed in victory (183). As Catholics, both time travellers are suspected of being Royalist spies. When challenged by a parliamentarian captain, John's illiteracy prevents him from reading and signing the papers put before him and he is unable to save William from the gallows.

Exeter Cathedral lies neglected in 1744, and the priests John encounters seem dissolute. By 1843, John claims to have lost everything – his wife, his baby son, his brother, all his possessions – and even his faith had been taken away from him by Henry VIII. He feels he has lost his place in time and seems to be contemplating hurling himself in the fast-flowing waters of the river when the kindly local vicar, Father Harington, accosts him and asks for a day to try to persuade him not to kill himself. Having travelled through four centuries, John feels he has seen 'all Christian life laid out' and it has left a bitter taste in his mouth (293). He repeats a Latin dictum: *Homi hominum daemon*, which translates as 'Man is a devil to man.' He had first used this saying after he had been whipped for challenging the priests in 1744. Reading the accumulated experiences of John as a Catholic traveller through time, I cannot avoid asking whether I can blame John for reaching this conclusion. Is it not a fair summary of the story of religion in Britain?

John's first experience of theatre comes in 1843 when Harington takes him to see *Doctor Faustus*. Of course, John sees himself in Faust on stage. He sees his and William's fate played out before his eyes, and this reopens the question of the genesis of his travels: did God, conscience or the devil offer him a different way to explore how to save his soul? Did John make a pact with the devil? Did he sell his soul?

John's sixth day is one of the last days of 1942, and John goes to the cinema while Exeter is under air attack. The cathedral looks as if it has survived bombings unscathed, but closer inspection reveals that all the windows are shattered and the old building is, in fact, ruined (339). Is this tattered cathedral an emblem of religion's fate in Britain after the painful centuries it has passed through?

The Outcasts of Time raises some challenging questions. I hold the view that text inserted or embedded in novels, whether citations of actual text or fictional, is often of great importance to the author and significant to any analysis of the book. So, in the Victorian section of Mortimer's book, my attention is drawn to two passages purportedly quoting a fictional book entitled *A Brief Enquiry into the Eternal Soul of Mankind*, which Harington chooses to read to John. They are about the study of the past and they ask whether it is preferable 'to have a blurred vision of all of the human past, or a clear one of a tiny particle of mankind's experience' (324). Is it better to be an expert in one subject only or jack of all trades? John avers that anyone who has no knowledge of the past lacks wisdom, then Harington quotes the book again saying that 'if we wish to understand our own place on earth, we must seek to understand those who have gone on before us' (325). Here, Mortimer puts a strong argument for the existence and value of historical fiction.

Again, my analysis of this novel has brought to the foreground the religious history told within it, but I wonder whether, before being a religious novel, *The Outcasts of Time* is primarily a moral novel. Is its primary aim to encourage us to save our souls by doing good deeds, as John sets out to do, or does it stand as an encouragement simply and non-religiously to do good things and cherish the good we do? In this sense, the novel can be read as a humanist text: we are better than we think we are. Yes, Britain is at war with France, with itself or with Germany in every year John visits, and religion is either the cause of the war or helpless in the face of the war, but John learns that what really matters is what does not change: the human spirit.

> At the end of the day. . . . What is important is what does not change – that mothers and wives are so happy when they hear that their sons and husbands are alive and run around the house yelling for joy; that men do their duty in the face of great danger not purely for themselves but for all their community. I am touched by these people's strength of spirit, which is as great as ever it was in my day (370).

We can comfort each other, even when the cathedrals and other edifices of society lie in ruins, and the novel ultimately shows that John can 'sow the seed' for generations of good people. The lessons John learns counter any pessimism left by the history of religion depicted in *The Outcasts of Time*.

Geraldine Brooks's *People of the Book* (2008) shifts time in the opposite direction, travelling back in time from when a book undergoes conservation in modern-day Sarajevo to the era of its origins. *People of the Book* is more clearly a religious novel than *The Outcasts of Time* in that its subject is an actual religious artefact, the Sarajevo Haggadah, the story of whose almost miraculous survival is uncovered by its conservator as she follows clues she finds in the book. Brooks does with the Sarajevo Haggadah what Neil MacGregor and the British Museum have done with some of the museum's artefacts in a radio series, *A History of the World in 100 Objects* (2015), and an exhibition, 'Living with the Gods' (2017-18): she uses it to uncover and trace a human story.

In the spring of 1996, the United Nations engages Hanna Heath to conserve the Haggadah, a codex telling the story of the Hebrews' escape from Egypt and typically used at Passover meals. When she explains what this conservation will entail, similarities with the work of historians and historical novelist become apparent: she will not restore it to its original condition for that shows no respect for the artefact. She sees her role as making the codex stable enough for future study and handling, repairing only when necessary. To explain this, she points out a dark red stain on one of the pages that she guesses is wine. She will analyse the stain because she may be able to determine where the book was when this stain was caused, and, if she is unable to do this now, she will leave it because technological developments in future years might help future conservators do the detective work (17). In fact, her investigation of this wine stain places the Haggadah in Venice in the first decade of the seventeenth century. Her work as a conservator compares with that of the historian and the historical novelist inasmuch as all three professions are focused on the evidence, to which they must remain faithful and which they do not want to destroy, and they use that evidence to fund imagination to recreate a form of the past. New readings of the evidence may yet, in future, give fresh expressions of that past.

Three book-centred faiths meet in *People of the Book*: Judaism, Islam and Christianity. Their styling as the Abrahamic faiths is occasionally disputed, but their close relationship, which I, as a Christian minister living and working in a city where many faiths and creeds collide, am keen to preserve, is apparent in this novel. They are not only 'cousins', who at various stages over the years have fallen out with each other, but they share a belief in the centrality of their scriptures. Jews, Muslims and Christians, in their different ways, are all people of their books. Relations between those faiths are never easy in the novel: when Ozren, the local man, who shows Hanna the Haggadah when she first arrives in Sarajevo, takes her to visit his three-year-old son who is seriously ill in hospital, they argue fiercely. Ozren vehemently refuses to get a second medical opinion so Hanna says, 'That's funny. I would never have picked you out as a believer in that bullshit, *insha'Allah*, fatalist mentality.' Ozren later regrets his outburst, but it illustrates the gulf between faiths:

> You are the one who is consumed by bullshit . . . all of you from the safe world. . . . You are the superstitious ones. You convince yourself that you can cheat death, and you are absolutely offended when you find you can't. . . . Bad things happen. Some very bad things happened to me. I live with it. Not every story has a happy ending. Grow *up*, Hanna, and accept that (37).

Once Hanna starts work on the Haggadah, she discovers clues on its pages and within its bindings. From these she is able to deduce where the codex has been over the centuries since it was first produced in Seville around 1480. She imaginatively recreates the story of the Haggadah. Her first stop back in time is Sarajevo in 1940 during the Nazi occupation of Bosnia. A fragment of a butterfly wing trapped in the binding sparks the recreation of the story of a young Jewish girl whom a Muslim family helps to flee Nazi oppression. The family also smuggles out the precious Haggadah. On her next stop back in time, in antisemitic Vienna towards the end of the nineteenth century, an unscrupulous Jewish bookbinder uses the delicate silver clasps in the style of feathers and a rose to pay for serum to treat his syphilis. The wine stains on the pages take us back to Venice in 1609 where the custodian of the Haggadah is Judah Aryeh. He acts on behalf of a noblewoman who has feigned conversion to Christianity to keep herself safe. Since 1589, when Pope Sixtus V banned all Jewish or Muslim books that contradicted the Catholic faith, priests had acted as book censors. Aryeh hopes his friendship with a priest will help to preserve the Haggadah from destruction and he tries to persuade that friend, Father Vistorini, to pass it. They agree nothing in the text would condemn it to the heresy pile, but the illustrations for the creation story in Genesis are another matter. Vistorini admires the first few illustrations, but the later ones troublingly depict the Earth as an orb. Both Vistorini and Aryeh know that most theologians no longer thought of the Earth as flat, but the problem was that the illustrator had put a second gold-leafed orb in the top-right corner of three pictures. In Vistorini's view this implied 'the heliocentric heresy' (184) and Vistorini is given to condemn the book – or, at least, remove the four offending pages. Wine had been taken during this conversation and it had been spilt. The entertaining story of how the Haggadah nevertheless survives, minus these four pages of illustrations, forms the remainder of this section.

Saltwater stains on the pages take readers further back in time to Tarragona in 1492 where the Inquisition tries to root out 'false *conversos* . . . who pollute the church with [their] lying presence' (231), but the saltwater is evidence that the Inquisition was unable to enforce Catholic orthodoxy, for the water was accidentally splashed on the Haggadah when a boy born to a Gentile was Judaised by full immersion. The final step back in time, by means of a white hair that proves to be a cat's hair from the paintbrush used to make the illustrations, is to the year the book was made: Seville, 1480. The three Abrahamic faiths converge here: the Haggadah is based on the Christian Book of Hours and the artist is a Muslim, who explains how a Muslim can be an illustrator when Islam frowns on images. He writes,

> The Jews, it seems, are as reluctant to make images as we Muslims are. But as I considered Benjamin, in his silence, shut out of understanding the beautiful and moving ceremonies of his faith, I remembered Isabella's prayer book, and the figures

in it, and how it helped her to pray. The idea came to me that such drawings would be of like help to Benjamin. I cannot think the doctor or his God will be offended by my pictures (314).

Brooks's novel gives a strong sense of the beauty of the Sarajevo Haggadah. In any theological treatise exploring God in any of the arts – music, painting, architecture, media, literature, sculpture and so on – beauty will feature, for these arts, in their different ways, rely on aesthetics. The refrain of one of Percy Dearmer's hymns ends with a proclamation: 'God is good! God is truth! God is beauty! Praise him!' Of the three theological assertions in the refrain, the assertion afforded least attention by theologians and preachers is 'God is beauty.' If God is beauty, Brooks's novel leads me to ask how beauty functions in the Christian faith. In what ways can art be an aid to prayer? How can art bolster belief? How can art illuminate truth? The novel also reminds me, because of its Middle Eastern setting, that other faiths eschew imagery and have an alternative understanding of beauty. For them, perhaps beauty is order and pattern. There is likely to be something for Christians to learn from these alternative views.

The various narratives in *People of the Book* effectively tell a version of the Jewish story from 1480 to the present age and demonstrate the sacrifices and obsessions that often lie behind religious belief. Above all, the depiction of religion in the book represents the violence resulting from religious intolerance, but, as Jennifer Wallace in her *Times Literary Supplement* review wrote, Brooks never denies the possibility of friendly gestures across the divisions.

My brief account of what happens in the eras visited in this novel does no justice to its breadth. There is much else of interest in *People of the Book* other than what the transmission of the Haggadah through the centuries tells about religious history. Readers can derive great enjoyment from following the forensic nature of Hanna's detective work and how she juggles that work with her private life. Yet, for Christian readers or people who read religiously, the book within the book, the Haggadah within *People of the Book*, bears witness to what Hanna's colleague and old postdoc friend, Raz, calls 'the human disaster' of the religious story when fear, hatred and a felt need to demonise the other rear up to smash society's potential for harmony (195).

Beth Underdown's debut novel, *The Witchfinder's Sister* (2017), like its less adventurous predecessor, Ronald Bassett's *Witchfinder General* (1966), which was brought to a wider audience when a film based on the book was released in 1968, is an example of historical fiction weaving a narrative around the barebones of an actual historical figure, Matthew Hopkins, a notorious seventeenth-century witchfinder. In modern terms, he was a serial killer. The author's note, which follows the main text, indicates that there are significant gaps in what is known about Hopkins, and that Underdown speculates on the probabilities in those gaps. It is probable that his father married only once, but Underdown gives Matthew a stepmother; it is not known whether he had a sister although he may have done, because it is known he had siblings, yet Underdown makes this possible sister the novel's narrator and protagonist; it is known that Matthew did not study theology at Cambridge and Underdown invents a reason why; and, while it is probable that Matthew died of consumption, she gives him an entirely different end. The Matthew Hopkins at the centre of this novel is merely based on the actual man of the past. Underdown, however, draws on assize records and pamphlets of the time, some of which she reproduces between chapters, including those of a minister who wrote in objection to Matthew's methods. Other improbable aspects of the novel's narrative, such as Rebecca West testifying against her own mother in a trial for witchcraft, is, on the other hand, true. Underdown's key source, John Stearne, is given only a small part in the novel.

Using a text from the book of Exodus and another from the Gospel of Matthew as epigraphs, and having a short foreword declaring that the English Civil War was a war about God and how best God should be worshipped, means that readers are confronted from the outset with the religious nature of this novel. Alice Hopkins's announcement that she will tell a tale she wishes were not true is an early indication that the religion explored here is problematic, perhaps unpleasant and dangerous. Yet she will record the whole sad business because, she says, the reasons Matthew had for what he did are to be unearthed in the past: 'I have learned that the acknowledged history that belongs to the daylight, that is not the only history. Turn over the stone and you will find another history, wriggling to escape' (6). Moreover, the novel will reveal a previously buried history of the real treatment of women whose behaviour is seen as troublesome.

The novel's action begins when Alice returns to be with her brother after the deaths of her mother and husband, and discovers that there has been talk of witchcraft in the region. Alice knows that such superstitious talk was once common among village folk, and that her father had frowned on any in his congregation who had indulged in it (50). Yet she is surprised to learn that Matthew is much less dismissive. Alice witnesses systematic witch hunting, with accusations made against women for a range of spurious reasons including demented or antisocial behaviour, harsh words and unexplained coincidences. Any one of these could be without foundation and Alice believes that none of those charged as witches were in any sense guilty (169). In a central passage she discusses the matter with her brother using experience, scripture and reason to bolster her argument. She begins by telling a story from her own experience that reverses the scenario. It is the story of a man who believed himself to be angel-possessed. He would sit on the mounting block by the inn and tell any person who walked past when they were going to die. She did not know whether he was ever correct in his predictions because he always gave distant future dates. Matthew's immediate opinion is that the man was devil-possessed. So Alice asks him why God has any need for witches if God can 'send the devil to us direct' (171). She also cites the biblical story of Simon Magus whom Peter, in Acts 8:9-24, confronted with the effect of leading him to conversion and baptism. In contrast, Matthew will not seek the redemption of witches, for other biblical texts such as Exodus 22:8 are clear in their condemnation of witchery. Little will deter him from identifying a woman as a witch. For example, after Susanna Smith's nurse tells him that a physician had diagnosed Susanna as brainsick, Matthew's response is unsympathetic and unyielding: 'I do not believe in brainsickness. She is entirely the devil's creature' (244).

The Witchfinder's Sister is not merely a straight account of conflict between religion and superstition. For his entire life Matthew has been sold a lie to mask the identity of his abuser, and this has led him always to confuse fiction with fact. Yet the novel is more than an account of confusion over what distinguishes fact from fiction. Alice, although she challenges her brother's opinions and activities, is a woman of her time sensing malign entities where they may be none and fearing anything extraordinary. Superstition was difficult to avoid in a pre-scientific age. Alice believes her brother was a monster, but, also, that it cannot be as simple as that (343). She is ultimately firm in her belief that 'evil does touch our mortal lives from time to time, but not, I am given to think, in such a way as can be explained. Not, perhaps, in such a way as it is possible to know who to blame' (343). We might ask if this rings true in contemporary experience, and, if so, is Alice correct to suggest that the choice we face is that between opening and closing our hearts?

When considering the motivations for Matthew's behaviour it is clear that his psychological makeup is complicated by the manner in which the true cause of the lifelong injuries he received as a baby has been hidden from him so that he has been allowed to believe an entirely false account. The novel, however, implies he may also have other motives. Perhaps he is simply a biblical literalist who takes as divine instruction the texts he has marked in his Bible, in Exodus, Deuteronomy, Leviticus and Samuel (210). Related to this, he declares himself a duteous servant who owes it to God 'to do his work with as much thoroughness as he can' (275). Perhaps all believers of his age saw the cleansing of all unrighteousness as their legitimate and divine calling. We might recall that a former servant in his parent's household, Sarah, speaks of him as a strange child who was 'never one to forgive a slight' (269). Quite apart from the effects of his childhood trauma, perhaps Matthew shows no signs of empathy and no signs of having a forgiving nature anywhere in the novel. When we look at how he treats Alice in the end, perhaps sheer wickedness motivates him and his religious fundamentalism masks misogyny.

Finally, we turn to one of the most popular historical novels of recent years: Sarah Perry's *The Essex Serpent*. Like *The Witchfinder's Sister*, it is based on an actual documented past, in this case a pamphlet originally published in 1669 warning the villagers of Henham-on-the-Mount, fictionalised in the novel as Aldwinter, that a sea monster is at large. The novel weaves an imagined narrative around the pamphlet to complete its, so-far only half-told, tale. A book covering four seasons, the novel has four parts, each given a title taken from the original pamphlet, and the events all occur within a year of one New Year's Day in the late nineteenth century when the tide threw up the body of a man with a broken neck. The cause of his death remains unexplained and this mystery revives rumours, which had lain dormant since the 1660s, of an Essex serpent terrorising the coastline. The re-emergence of the monster appears to have been coincidental with an earthquake in the region.

At the funeral of one Michael Seaborne, readers are introduced to his feisty widow, Cora, who has an interest in palaeontology, a very popular pastime of the period. Her widowhood has liberated her and, in the company of her close friend, Martha, she visits Colchester where a chance meeting with one of her late husband's former colleagues leads to his writing a letter introducing her to the rector of Aldwinter. Receipt of this letter irritates Revd William Ransome, for he is trying to quell the rumours of what he chooses to refer to as 'The Trouble'. He hopes that, by refusing to name the serpent, he will defuse the situation, and that Cora's fresh interest in the story from outside the village will not give it added credence. Cora's several meetings with local people, such as her encounter with a farmer hanging dead moles on fences to scare moles from his fields – a practice I witnessed only four or five years ago when walking in Cumbria – and an account of the rector's children re-enacting a ritual in honour of the goddess Persephone, indicate how difficult it would be for the rector to squash rumours of the serpent. The world in which he ministers is full of folklore, superstition and unorthodox rituals, a world full of people hungry for tales of the unknown.

There is a sense in which the novel depicts a church assailed on two sides. From one side, it is challenged by the remnants of folk religion represented by villagers such as Cracknell and Banks, while from the other, it is challenged by developing sciences such as evolutionary theory, Martha's socialism, and advances in medicine, surgery and hypnosis. None of these is set in direct opposition to another; it is not a straightforward matter of good religion versus bad superstition, or of modern science replacing outdated religion. Rather, they coexist in tension. Take, for instance, Martha's political interest in housing the poor. Perry gives an almost religious quality to her political faith: 'Community halls and picket lines were [Martha's] temples, and Annie Besant and Eleanor Marx stood at the altar: she had no hymn book but the fury of folk songs setting English suffering to English melody' (107). Is she implying that this is a more effective alternative than religion for the betterment of humanity? Perry presents Will's faith, on the other hand, as being no more effectual than being capable of holding things together, rather than improving the human lot: he holds 'a common faith overlooked by a benevolent God that will keep the fabric of society from tearing' (49). Under-occupied in the parish of Aldwinter, Will takes his Sunday duties seriously, but 'His was not the kind of religion lived only in rule and rubric, as if he were a civil servant and God the permanent secretary of a celestial government department. He felt his faith deeply, and above all out of doors, where the vaulted sky was his cathedral nave and the oaks its transept pillars' (113). I suspect that Perry, while respecting this character, is nevertheless indicating that his form of Christianity and churchmanship lacks fervour, direction and power. Thinking deeply about matters of faith leads him to write to Cora. He tells her that someone has been hanging horseshoes in Traitor's Oak, presumably to ward off some form of evil, and one of the farmer's crops has been burned. Will is at a loss and wonders if the village is under judgment, then how the villagers can atone for whatever they have done wrong. He feels that his efforts to be a good pastor to the village are being thwarted by circumstance. Yet he refuses to compromise: 'I won't accept my faith is the faith of superstition,' he writes. 'But it's a faith of reason, not darkness: the Enlightenment did away with all that. If a reasoned Creator set the stars in their place then we must be capable of understanding them – we must also be creatures of reason, of order!' (258). He believes there must be a rational and scientific explanation for the strange events in the village, whereas Cora harbours a less pragmatic theory that creatures from the ancient past, capable of wreaking havoc, might somehow have survived into the present.

One April day when they walk together to World's End (where else?), Will and Cora share what we might call a mystical experience. Here is Perry's account:

> They reached the water – the tide was out – mud and shingle gleamed in the westering light. . . . Neither was ever certain who first shielded their eyes against the dazzle on the water, and saw what lay beyond. Neither recalled having exclaimed, or having told the other 'Look – look!' only that all at once both stood transfixed on the path above the saltings, gazing east. There on the horizon, between the silver line of water and the sky, there lay a strip of pale and gauzy air. Within the strip, sailing far above the water, a barge moved slowly through the lower sky. It was possible to make out the separate pieces of its oxblood sail, which appeared to move under a strong wind; there quite clearly was the deck and the rigging, the dark prow. On it went, flying in full sail, high above the estuary; it flickered, and diminished, then regained its size; then for a moment it was possible to see the image of it inverted just beneath, as if a great mirror had been laid out. The air grew chill – the bittern boomed – each heard the other breathing swiftly, and it was not quite terror they felt, though something like it. Then the mirror vanished, and the boat sailed on alone; a gull flew below the black hull, above the gleaming water. Then some member of the ghostly crew tugged a rope, or dropped an anchor – the vessel ceased to move, only hung on silent, wonderful, becalmed against the sky. William Ransome and Cora Seaborne, stripped of code and convention, even of speech, stood with her strong hand on his: children of the earth and lost in wonder (169-70).

This is the moment when the two come closest to mutual acknowledgement of their love for one another. By using terms such as 'almost terror' and 'lost in wonder', Perry describes the moment as a form of religious experience, an experience of the numinous that Rudolf Otto called *mysterium tremendum et fascinans*. Later, however, Will writes to Cora and explains the experience as a Fata Morgana illusion. Such illusions are named after a fairy, Morgan le Fay, who, siren-like, bewitched sailors to their deaths by building icy castles in the air above the sea to delude them. The scientific, or, as Will calls it, the 'prosaic', explanation of Fata Morgana illusions is that 'a particular arrangement of cold and warm air creates a refracting lens. The light which reaches the observer is bent upward in such a way that objects beneath or beyond the horizon are refracted far above their location. . . . Objects are not only misplaced, but repeated and distorted.' He concludes that their 'senses were deceived utterly – we stood for a moment clean out of our wits, as though our bodies conspired against our reason' (172-3). Will is left distrusting the capacity of his mind to interpret what his eyes see.

Allusions to a verse from Hebrews 11 occur at several points in the novel: it speaks of faith as 'the substance of things hoped for and the conviction of things not seen' (374). This text problematises the concepts of delusion and illusion. If faith lends its realising light (to quote the hymn writer, Charles Wesley) and realises, or makes real, something that is unseen, does this mean that faith authenticates something illusory or false? In the borderlands between religion and superstition, what is the difference between crossing one's fingers or touching wood for luck and praying? Many contemporary sportspeople display a range of rituals that some will describe as religious and others will dismiss as superstitious. Famous tennis players adopt compulsive rituals prior to playing and footballers cross themselves before taking a penalty kick. Can there be any genuine religious purpose to such practices?

The entire novel concerns this distinction between reality and illusion. Indeed, what, after all, is the eponymous Essex serpent? Is it the insidious presence of two of the mortal sins besetting the characters, namely lust and jealousy? Is it the insidious effect of delusion and illusion on people's sanity, perception and lives? Or is it the insidious result of ignorance and poor education? Perhaps Perry implies it is something of each of these, as she notes that, after the excitement is over and the mystery removed, Will preaches a sermon in which his references to the serpent – their false fear of it and the double illusion of it, all of which had upset their locality – are concealed 'in a kindly homily regarding Eden's garden' (414). In a subversion of the conventional practice of preaching that is intended to be revelatory, Will hides the reality behind warm words!

My readings of these four novels, which I suggest are representative of the historical novel genre in recent years, convince me not only that historical novelists use religion as a tool for setting contexts for their narratives, thus capturing the spirit of their eras, but also that religion, spirituality and theology thereby become matters for debate within the books. These novels show that religion is an active vital force, and not simply an historical phenomenon. Furthermore, the depiction of religion in historical novels reminds contemporary Christian readers that all expressions of Christianity are unavoidably time-bound and contextualised. I suspect, therefore, that this serves to remind the contemporary church that, if the Christian faith is to continue to be a vibrant living faith, Christians should be prepared to change and adapt to the age they claim to serve.

Chapter 6
HISTORICAL DETECTIVE FICTION

Within the genre of historical fiction there is a subgenre, that of historical detective fiction, meriting separate attention.

Since 1910 when G.K. Chesterton introduced Father Brown to the readers of the world, detective fiction has almost universally highlighted traditional morality and Christian orthodoxy.[1] Indeed, all detective fiction may have always had a close relationship with religious faith and practices, for possibly no other literary genre is as morally orthodox as the detective story. Detective stories are predicated on the commitment of crime, the pursuit of the criminal and the assumption of punishment. One literary critic, Robert S. Paul, argued that the appeal of detective fiction lies in the implicit morality that readers unconsciously affirm, and he suggests that the presuppositions, without which detective fiction would be unable to function, are all fundamentally theological. There are at least seven such presuppositions: first, the belief that rational, presumably God-given, laws govern the universe; second, the conviction that truth can be discovered by rationally weighing the evidence, and, in the case of detective fiction, the truth under investigation is the truth hidden within a crime scene; third, the assumption that, if all facts are known, meaning can be discovered in them; fourth, the perception that there is a real discernible difference between right and wrong conduct, and usually right conduct is valued more highly; fifth, the assumption that human life is of supreme value and to be honoured above all else, an assumption enshrined in the fifth of the Ten Commandments; sixth, the recognition that all people are capable of both good and evil actions; and, finally, the conviction that, for the good of human society, all people must seek to establish justice, and to this end those who investigate crime and pursue criminals are on the side of the angels.[2]

1. Kim, (2005), p. 5.
2. *ibid.*, p. 6.

In other words, detective fiction is predicated on there being a moral universe. It need not be essentially theological in nature, but in much detective fiction there is a frequent incidence of religious institutions as crime settings, and of priests and monks as amateur sleuths. Recently, James Runcie's Sidney Chambers has joined a distinguished line of religious investigators among whom the best-known are Father Brown, Cadfael and Brother William of Baskerville.

In 2012, Runcie, the son of the late Archbishop of Canterbury, began this popular detective series featuring the newly ordained vicar of Grantchester, who teams up with Inspector Geordie Keating to combat crime in the parish. The series reveals the author's access to insider knowledge regarding the role of parish priests, even to the point of their exasperation with the common perception that Christmas is their busy time of year. He must have watched his father carefully. The first in the series, *Sidney Chambers and the Shadow of Death*, takes the form of six short episodes, in each of which Chambers solves a mystery including a suspected suicide, a jewellery theft, an unexplained death and an art forgery. Often these leave him questioning the nature of his vocation. 'He had not undertaken Holy Orders so that he could consort with policemen and threaten doctors. . . . He had a bounden duty to exercise care and diligence in bringing those in his charge to the faith and knowledge of God' (192).

Other characters often make assumptions about Chambers – that he will prefer to drink sherry before any other beverage, that he will be chaste if not married, that he will be intolerant of homosexuality and that God will be on his side, not only when playing backgammon (which he plays weekly in the pub with Keating), but also in the game of life. He colludes with none of these, but he does collude with the assumption of round-the-clock availability. A knock on the door or the telephone bell could, at any time, interrupt other duties with either an urgent or a trivial matter, and Chambers always feels duty-bound to respond.

The rack on which Chambers is gently tortured (the oxymoron is intentional) is evident when he preaches. George Herbert, poet-priest of the seventeenth century, described vocation both as a restraining collar and a rack that pulled him apart, but the stress and strain that Chambers feels as he collaborates with Inspector Keating in the pursuit of offenders in his parish is rarely of high intensity: 'He looked down from the pulpit and realised he was not able to reach every parishioner. The elderly looked benevolent and grateful, but younger widows from the war carried a grief that could not be assuaged. . . . He wished, once more, that he could be a better priest' (206). Although set in the 1950s, this series of books can offer insights into the life of parish clergy in the twenty-first century, including the important question that Chambers asks so publicly – whether an always available priest is a 'better' priest.

Reaching back further into the past than Runcie's Grantchester Mysteries, Samantha Harvey's *The Western Wind* (2018) is a late medieval mystery, set in the fictional isolated Midlands village of Oakham. In the absence of any other local officials, it falls on the village's priest, John Reve, to serve as judge, chief investigator and sheriff to unravel the mystery of how the richest man in the village, Thomas Newman, died. At the beginning of the novel, Herry Carter rouses Reve from his confession booth and takes him to where he has found a body in the river, but the corpse has disappeared, presumably swept further downstream. All that remains is Newman's shirt left hanging on a tree, and they find a dead dog where they believe Newman had entered the water.

The rural dean has been sent to the village to ensure there is a proper investigation, but he is more concerned to find an explanation swiftly than find out what really happened, and he encourages Reve, by hearing as many confessions as he can, to identify the murderer so both the case and the culprit can be dispatched before Lent begins. Reve hears many a false confession between Shrove, or Egg, Saturday and Shrove Tuesday in February 1491. One villager, Robert Tunley, confesses to poisoning the dog because its barking and howling kept him awake at night; a maid, Marjory Smith, confesses that she has observed Lord Townshend mistreating his wife, sometimes tying her to the bedpost for hours; when Herry Carter falsely confesses to the murder, Reve attributes his confusion to the pain and poison of a festering head wound; on his second attempt to confess, Carter, although he thinks Newman could still be alive because his body has not been found, expresses his belief that he had killed Newman because he had disappointed him (113). Suspicion soon falls on Lord Townshend because Newman had been buying up his land. While Newman had been getting richer, Townshend had seen his fortunes diminish. The dean is keen to lay the blame on Townshend and tries to force Reve to accept the false confessions he has overheard (79).

Because Reve's confessional is the scene for most of his investigations, penance and mercy are recurring theological themes in *The Western Wind*, themes personified in the figure of Piers Kemp, the miller. When Reve sees him 'hobbling his pained way back from Newman's house with his shoes filled with stones' (57), the miller greets him jauntily even though he hobbles on stones at the will of the priest. Reve comments that mercy seemed strange to him because it took such outwardly unmerciful forms.

Mercifully, I might ironically say, Piers Kemp has less distance to walk than the travellers Reve had encountered four summers previously: they were walking to Rome, Santiago de Compostela, France, then home. Each confession Reve hears ends with a required penance, calculated to satisfy the expectations of the penitent who, like a modern-day patient consulting a GP who feels the consultation has reached a satisfactory conclusion when he or she receives a prescription, leaves the confessional with something to help the problem. For instance, Herry Carter thinks his penance is to shrive the murder he has confessed, but Reve knows it is to shrive the sin of falsely confessing to murder: 'What did it matter, so long as it was a penance [Carter] found sufficiently dangerous, cold, bleak and thankless . . . something that could make him feel he was punishing himself, until he'd punished himself enough' (114). The timing of the novel's action, in the last days before the annual self-denial of Lent begins, makes the villagers' need to make penance more acute and their sense of a merciful God more distant as the mysterious scandal blights the village.

Being both chief investigator and the novel's narrator, Reve's self-awareness is never far from the reader's gaze. His unique status in the village requires him to tread carefully along a line on which he can be both intimate, as a trusted friend and confidant, and distant as Christ's vicar in Oakham. He shows great empathy for the villagers, even for those who are less than appealing in nature, but he is often riven with doubt about his abilities and his vocation. Keen to protect Townshend from false accusation because the dean wants to pin responsibility for Newman's death on him, Reve is not so holy that he will not tamper with the evidence: he helps Carter hide the potentially incriminating shirt (246). The novel offers an incidental analysis of priestly vocation that is tested in a bizarre experiment carried out annually on Shrove Sunday to assess the priest's suitability to lead the village into Lent. Someone of similar size to the priest is selected and, before a crowd of two-thirds of the village, each steps into a boat pulled parallel to the bank and sits at opposite ends. If Reve's end of the boat sinks lower into the water than the other end, this indicates that Reve weighs less, and weighing less than a man whose build was similar was seen to denote his 'ongoing priestliness' (204). He was deemed to weigh more than an angel, but less than a man. Later, Reve writes of being anointed at ordination as light for the world, while being only a man like other men whose muscles ache and whose eyes blur with sleep (210). He speaks of being a golden hook, which is an image one of the villagers named Agnes Prye had used earlier to describe his role. Wanting to say that Reve is more than an ordinary man, she describes the priest as 'the Ghostly Father, him between us and the

Lord. . . . The golden hook . . . to catch all the fish' (97). He corrects her: as *primus inter pares*, he says, he is 'chief parishioner', therefore a villager like the others. She insists on seeing him as 'higher than the angels' (98), but Reve knows otherwise: he had grown up thinking that the only way to show the truth of one's faith was to be able to summon the wind at will. One day, he hopes he would demonstrate 'the ultimate standard of [his] closeness to God' by bringing a wind from the west simply because he asked and for no better reason. He would tell no one of this private barter because he doubted the veracity of his life's vocation (134). Truthfully, however, the integrity of his vocation does not depend on his ability to achieve this impossibility; it depends on his faithful service to the church and the village it serves.

On Shrove Monday, also known as Collop Monday, Reve, feeling the whole weight of the village on his shoulders, hurries to the church. On his way, he glimpses what he thinks is a 'were-creature', and, panicked, he rushes through the churchyard. Peace only returns after entering the church. Unable to pray, he sits on a stool, and, gazing around the nave, he recalls his ordination, since when he has been a man trying to do an angel's work (138). Like St Christopher, whose image carrying the child Jesus over the river is depicted on the wall of the church, Reve realises that over time, because of his duties as a priest, he will carry each and every soul in the parish across the breach from death into the next world. What plagues him now is that he has not assisted Newman across the divide. In his disappointment and agony, the church affords Reve no shelter, but is 'a darkness inside a bigger darkness' (139), and he expresses himself suspicious of such emptiness.

Judge, sheriff, vicar, light of the world, chief investigator, seeker after truth, heavier than an angel and called to do the work of angels, Reve is a mere man. The burden of his calling weighs heavy on him:

> Your priestly duties will strain you, I was told in my training. You'll feel like a bow whose string is pulled back and back until your flex is used up and you feel you can't flex more. . . . But if you wait, you'll learn that this flexing is in order for the arrow to fly, which is the part of you that belongs with the Lord and is directed towards him, finely fletched and shooting fair (285).

The exercise of ministry does indeed test elasticity, especially when it is exercised among people such as the people of Oakham. Oakham is a village of 'scrags and outcasts', a village that had come to no good, not able to trade in wool, incapable of making cloth and without the skill to build the bridge it so desperately needs to escape its isolated location on the wrong side of a bend in the river (102). Villagers do silly, inexplicable things such as covering the naked body of Christ on a crucifix by wrapping a shawl around his shoulders and a frilled skirt around his waist to keep him warm in Lent, thereby leaving Christ looking like a clown. Such behaviour, perhaps indicating misplaced spirituality or long-term moral collapse, as well as ignorance and foolishness, exasperates Reve. Nevertheless, one reviewer, M. John Harrison, described *The Western Wind* as a novel about the grace we find in people.[3] Perhaps we discover this grace primarily in Reve himself and in his patient empathy with the sometimes graceless people to whom he ministers.

The novel provides a good example of the way detective fiction is based on fundamentally theological presuppositions about the moral universe in that its narrator and its characters assume that God orders the universe. Even so, humankind can neither manipulate nor control this God: Lady Townshend, in her understandable impatience to protect her husband and in her loving desire to ensure the heavenly destiny of her lover, presses ten pounds into Reve's hand, saying, 'This is my prayer. . . . Let God know I've donated it and ask him to give Thomas Newman a place in heaven' (171). Reve knows the generosity of the donation will make no difference: God can be neither bribed nor coerced. Throughout, characters share certainty that life is no more than a prelude to eternity, and their various confessions prepare their way after misdemeanours in this life, yet Harvey roots her unorthodox detective novel in the quiddity, the whatness or thisness, of earthy rural village life on the banks of a bridgeless river. Harvey makes us aware of the transitory nature of happiness in medieval England, and the spirituality of her characters' lives is earthed in the ordinary stuff of life. For instance, when Reve patiently waits in his confession box for the next parishioner to list his or her sins, he feels his heartbeat and reflects on the fact that one day his heart will stop. He wonders what will be in store for him, and, while readers expect thoughts of eternity, Reve's thoughts are much more mundane: he realises he has forgotten to eat and is hungry.

Reve reports two sermons he preaches during these four days of investigation. The first, although the second chronologically, as the four days of the book are narrated in reverse order, is 'On the Lord's prudent and timely use of the wind' (116-18), an entertaining piece for readers for several reasons including its rhetoric, its exhortation for cleanliness, its immediate effect on the audience and the altar candles, and its use

---

3. In a review in *The Guardian*, 1 March 2018.

of a phoney visual aid. Reve begins by asking whether they have ever known a wetter winter. This winter has rotted food, drowned animals and raised a malicious air bearing maladies. He tells members of the congregation, who ask why God has let such pestilence and decay flourish, that God tests people. The slightest impurity – a morsel of rotted meat or the residue of sin in a person's heart – is sufficient to infect entire populations. Because God does not sweep everything clean, people must take some responsibility for their own lives: to prevent the stagnant Night Air bringing disease into their homes, villagers should sluice their floors, wash their bodies, cut their hair, tend their creatures, come to Mass, say their prayers and pay their tithes. If God sees that villagers make some effort, then perhaps God will match their efforts with God's own and send a fast wind to blow malicious spirits out to sea and clean the air. Because Reve knows parishioners will not want a fast wind because it will bend their brassicas diagonal and downcast their livestock, he waves before them a treatise entitled *On the Lord's Prudent and Timely Use of the Wind*. This shows how God can send wind not to punish, but to reward good work and rid places of 'corrupted vapours'. He alludes to the locust plague carried on an east wind in the Book of Joel, and announces that he is praying for a west wind that is the breath of God to blow Thomas Newman's soul out of this world and safely into the next. But, he says, villagers must play their part, keeping themselves and their homes clean, their animals tended, their tithes paid and their 'sins trivial and quickly confessed'. Thus, they will show that Oakham is a courageous and virtuous parish, doing its best to please God. The congregational 'Amen' that greeted the conclusion of the sermon raised a breath of air that caused the candles on the altar to gutter and 'bow dangerously deep' (118), the combined breath of the congregation being an immediate answer to Reve's prayer for a west wind. Someone in the congregation breaks wind as they rise to leave, as if God is in the breath, the words, the actions and the activity of villagers. They, too, must make efforts. As they leave the church, a conversation between Reve and the dean reveals that the treatise the preacher had held up was not what he had claimed it to be. It was his priest's manual. He defends himself: 'I know what I said was true, about the wind, the vapours, even if it's not written in a treatise' (118). His role as a preacher and pastor is to give his hearers hope, and, in his case, it seems by whatever means.

On the previous day, Quinquagesima Sunday, Reve had preached a sermon entitled 'On the Devil's Meddling with the Fickle Element of Music' asserting his authority in the parish and addressing his concern that many villagers were worried that the unshriven soul of Thomas

Newman was trapped earthbound and still stalking the village (178-80). Reve begins this sermon with a legend. He tells of a fisherman with a peculiar, but successful technique. After throwing his hook into the water and securing the line to his boat, he would lure fish to the hook by playing his harp. All was well until one winter day the devil rowed in on his boat and made a hissing sound that, as far as fish were concerned, was as airy and sweet as the fisherman's harp. The devil's nets were full, while the fisherman's were empty, and, after several days and weeks like this, the fisherman, his family and the villagers were rake-thin. All might have been lost, except that on one bright day, the sun caught something glinting in the bow of the boat. It was a golden hook. When he used this hook to fish, the fish left the devil and came back to him.

Reve asks who in his audience knows what the legend is about. Some in the congregation offer answers: is it about the devil being a gluttonous bastard? Is it about old Clere from Bourne who used to sell fish in Oakham but died of an ulcerous leg? Is it about one of Jesus's disciples? No, says Reve, none of these. The fisherman represents each of the villagers, for the story shows how the devil's music can creep in unless they use the golden hook to leave the devil hissing to himself, and their priest is the golden hook. Reve is God's worker among them.

He reminds them that Thomas Newman had spoken of the delightful airiness of music, which, because of its airiness, resonates with the human spirit and draws us heavenward. He had played his lute to demonstrate how music 'channel[led] cosmic influences' (179), a phrase none of them had understood. The rapture of sound, Newman had claimed, could raise them to the heavens. Reve disputes this and waves a treatise before his hearers that he says describes the duplicity of music, which, in spite of its loveliness, is susceptible to hell. Although music can be fair and free and like the breath of God, he claims that the subtle, shape-shifting devil can also come through music. Reve alone is the only safe channel to God: 'I am your golden hook: I am the one who can attract God's truth, so that those truths can nourish you' (180). He claims to be the person best placed to discern whether any music they hear is divine or diabolical: if it falls on Reve's ears it must come from God, and if that happens, he says as he brings his sermon to a conclusion, they can all rejoice that Newman's soul is winging and singing its way to heaven 'leav[ing] a delicate trail of sound, like the effervescence of a shooting star' (180). This is the second time Reve has held up a treatise for his congregation to see, and the fact that he thumbs the downy pages of his priest's manual as he watches the congregation leave at the end of the service implies that the manual has been his phoney visual aid once more.

The dean had stood at the back of the church throughout this sermon and had looked pleased. Reve tells readers what he thinks the dean would have thought of this sermon, thereby making his own critique. Its hectoring and chastening tone had reinforced the subordinate role of parishioners and lectured them on the merits of knowing their own ignorance. However, the whimsical reference to shooting stars would have jarred, for a warning on 'the perils of airiness' should not end with a notion of the stars. He and the dean seem pleased with the devotion displayed in the congregation's attention to prayer and its eager celebration of the Eucharist that follow the sermon.

Despite the novel's unorthodox structure telling the story in reverse, *The Western Wind* is an outstanding recent example of historical detective fiction in which several theological and religious themes enrich the mystery for Christian readers. First, in common with the Grantchester chronicles, it invites readers to consider the nature of the priestly vocation as the work of angels carried out by mere mortals. The parish priest is a golden hook drawing all that is of God to the village, and all that is godly in the village towards God. This lays a heavy burden on Reve's shoulders. Second, the novel includes a continuous dialogue with the reader on the relationship between mercy, penance and confession: to what extent does the mercy of God depend upon the making of confession and the performance of penitent acts? Or, to update the question to twenty-first-century expressions of morality and faith, to what extent does forgiveness rely upon penitence? Can a murderer experience forgiveness only after expressing regret? And how can a third party, such as a priest, communicate forgiveness when the priest has not been hurt by the perpetrator's actions? These questions relate to *The Western Wind*'s third theological theme: God's activity within the universe, and the extent to which the novel's characters sense that the world and their lives in it are where God is active. The views strongly held by the characters in the novel, that God orders the world and that their lives are preparation for eternity, are less common among its readers. Nevertheless, it is important to note when reading this novel that the genre of detective fiction relies on the presumption of such a moral universe, in which its characters, whether goodies or baddies, are subject to certain moral imperatives. Fourth, Reve's discussion of music in his Quinquagesima sermon brings to the fore the otherwise incidental theme of music in religion: how do we use it in worship? In what ways does music communicate to the human soul that which is of God? In characterising music as a tempter leading Christians off the true path, Reve is unconventional in his opinions, for only a small proportion of Christians have eschewed its use entirely. The more common view in Christianity is that music is not only God's gift, but fills the air of heaven, where, according to John Donne's prayer, there is no noise nor silence but one equal music. And the more common view in twenty-first-century Western society is that, through music, one human spirit communicates with another – player and listener in conversation – and that, even for the person who is not remotely religious, music speaks to the inner self. Music cannot be separated from human spirituality.

There are such rich theological themes in Harvey's novel because, in the absence of any other official investigating body, Harvey has chosen the parish priest as her chief investigator and narrator. Not only, as with other historical fiction, does the practice of religion establish the novel's historical context, but religious and spiritual themes follow from the nature of its central mystery within a moral universe – the death of a rich man who died with the burden of a confession still on his heart.

Chapter 7

ATHEIST NOVELS
'The quarrel over God'

Contemporary novels belong to a world often described as postmodern, which usually refers to the way in which any sense of an overarching narrative capable of accounting for the nature of existence in a comprehensive and satisfactory manner has broken down. Suspicion of authority prevails. No single account of existence can be adequate and the age is characterised by competing convictions. The contemporary Western world may thus be described as being more disputatious over God. Theism can no longer be the assumed norm. We live in a time when, in the opinion of Edward Mayhew, the protagonist in Ian McEwan's *On Chesil Beach*, 'religion ha[s] generally faded into insignificance' (45), except when corrupt forms of religion wreak havoc and create terror in society. Then it feels that religious belief is unparalleled in significance.

At the turn of the millennium, David McLaurin, author at that stage of his career of three novels, wrote an essay reflecting on his craft.[1] He began with the assertion that novels spring from the culture in which they are written, and any spiritual content they may have is born of that culture. His essay discussed morality and spirituality in *Manon Lescaut*, Jane Austen and Evelyn Waugh. That McLaurin felt he lived in a darker world of weaker faith than that of the Abbé Prévost, Austen and Waugh seems less than propitious for the future of novelistic discussions of morality, spirituality and faith.

Yet in 2013 this dark world of weak faith, as McLaurin called it, saw the inauguration of the Sunday Assembly, a church for atheists who, despite their non-belief, seek a church experience. Ironically or intentionally – I cannot be sure whether irony was intended or not – Sanderson Jones and Pippa Evans convened its first meeting in a disused church that retained the appearance and many of the features of a traditional church building. The Sunday Assembly continues to offer ritual, the communal

1. Published in Fiddes, (2000), pp. 61-76.

experience of community singing, aesthetics, humour, laughter and happiness, and an edifying, uplifting message all intended to be life-enhancing. A degree of surrealism hangs over this phenomenon, which must excite the curiosity of anthropologists and sociologists alike. The thriving existence of the Sunday Assembly also raises interesting questions for religionists. Does it imply that atheism on its own is a failing trend, that it lacks human essentials such as ritual, communal activities and shared experience of aesthetics? Is *homo religiosus* unable to live without some form of religion even if its ritual is bereft of any sense of divinity? What is the essential difference between an edifying speech and a sermon? Why, indeed, are some of Richard Dawkins's speeches and articles received as secular sermons?

And what if people in churches, mosques, synagogues and temples began to talk atheistically? In the last fifty years, some novelists have written atheistic sermons into their fiction. Carel Fisher, an eccentric rector of a bombed-out city church, in Iris Murdoch's *The Time of the Angels* (1966), contemplated beginning a sermon 'What if I told you there's no God?', and Carel's struggle with religious belief culminates in an anti-sermon he delivers to his faithful brother, Marcus. Three atheistic preachers feature in A.S. Byatt's Frederica quartet of novels: *The Virgin in the Garden* (1978), *Still Life* (1985), *Babel Tower* (1996) and *A Whistling Woman* (2002). There is an outspoken atheist, Bill Potter, who preaches an anti-sermon on the folly of belief in the virgin birth; his son-in-law Daniel Orton, a clergyman whose preaching is never described in the novels because, in the first of the series, he dismisses the practice of preaching as mere 'words, words'; and, in *A Whistling Woman*, Adelbert Holly whose sermons on St Lucy's Day and Christmas Day proclaim that 'God is not present. When Nietzsche declared that He had died, he described a state of affairs people recognised' (241). Among American writers, John Updike created a more notorious atheist preacher. In *A Month of Sundays* (1975), Updike used Thomas Marshfield's troubling and challenging sermons both to trace the course of his recuperation as he prepares to return to parish work, and to highlight incessant discontinuity between his life and work.

Bradley and Tate, in their introduction to New Atheist novels, argue that atheist writers use novels as a new frontline attack in the ideological war with religion, religious fundamentalism and religious terror. They go on to suggest that, in the view of such writers, the novel form 'offers a this-worldly experience of grandeur, consolation, freedom and even redemption'.[2] For some, in an age of declining organised religion and

2. Bradley and Tate, (2010), p. 11.

weak faith, the new religions are music, fine art, nature, sport, human camaraderie and literature, akin to the Wordsworthian 'sense and motion ... that rolls through all things', the sense sublime that Wordsworth met under a sycamore tree a few miles above Tintern Abbey. For this reason alone, atheist fiction cannot be ignored in this book. It, too, is a form of make-believe. In this chapter on novels written by atheists, I intend to show that secular literature oozes the sacred and that the Christian reader, perhaps when reading against the grain, can discern godliness in intended secularity.

Some Christian readers might be wary of dabbling in books that expose them to alternative worldviews and forms of religion, and they might be doubly cautious of turning to atheist writers. However, it will soon become apparent that such novelists rarely entirely avoid religious, theological or spiritual themes. They capture the *spirit* of postmodernity. Indeed, some atheist writers focus quite intensely on such themes. They are like Thomas in James Wood's *The Book against God* (2004), a character who is described as an atheist who cannot stop talking about God. *Make-Believe* would thus be incomplete if we did not explore what these unsympathetic writers say about God, and I believe Christian readers would impoverish themselves if they avoided such books. We turn, first, to Ian McEwan, whom Bradley and Tate introduce as the New Atheist novelist *par excellence*. A committed atheist, McEwan looks for transcendence in art, music and landscapes. He seeks secular transcendence in both the unintended and intentional atheology of fiction.

Saturday (2005) follows in the tradition of James Joyce's *Ulysses* (1922) and Virginia Woolf's *Mrs Dalloway* (1925) in that the novel anatomises a day in the life of its main character, Hugh Perowne, a neurosurgeon who plans on enjoying a day off that will culminate in a much-needed family reunion. The day, 15 February 2003, begins earlier than planned as, unable to sleep, Perowne stands at the window watching a burning plane descend over London into Heathrow. His mind, and ours, reach back to an actual event, the horrific sight, only seventeen months earlier, when hijackers sent two passenger aircraft into the twin towers of the World Trade Center. Such vivid memories evoked at the outset establish *Saturday* as a post-9/11 novel, providing space for dialogues about politics, society and morality: all events within the book, and, in particular, its portrait of religion, occur under the shadow of the terrorist act that did most, so far, to destabilise the twenty-first century. Perowne, whose earliest childhood memory was watching television coverage of the aftermath of the Aberfan disaster, when, in 1966, a coal waste tip slipped and overwhelmed a primary school in the South Wales valleys, killing 147 villagers, most of whom were children, now no longer believes in God. Watching reports of Aberfan on television was when he first suspected that the supposedly child-loving God of whom his teacher spoke did not exist: 'There is no entity for him to doubt' (32), and he thinks of his children's generation as a sincerely godless one. Yet he has named his son Theo, and, as he watches the burning plane, he wonders why it is in flames:

> A man of sound faith with a bomb in the heel of his shoe. Among the terrified passengers many might be praying – another problem of reference – to their own god for intercession. And if there are to be deaths, the very god who ordained them will soon be funereally petitioned for comfort. Perowne regards this as a matter of wonder, a human complication beyond the reach of morals. From it there spring, alongside the unreason and slaughter, decent people and good deeds, beautiful cathedrals, mosques, cantatas, poetry (17-18).

Almost the first thoughts in Perowne's day are thus religious, and they strike at the heart of the frustrating contribution of religion throughout human history: that which has the potential to benefit human society is also responsible for causing irrecoverable damage to it.

In interviews McEwan has said he subscribes to no supernatural beliefs, but acknowledges that 'the religious, or the numinous urge in people, is deeply stitched into human nature'.[3] Universals and whatever is common to human societies interest him more than differences, and he appreciates that religion is a strong feature across all human culture. Such religion, he says, has a core of dread, delight and transcendence. We should not be surprised, therefore, to find these elements discussed in his novels.

Perowne is incredibly ill-educated as far as the arts, and literature in particular, are concerned despite the efforts of his daughter, Daisy, who studies English literature at university. Can any person intelligent enough to be a neurosurgeon really know as little about books as Perowne? Unlike McEwan, who believes that fiction can capture the moral tangle of human existence, Perowne does not understand why anyone needs to make up stories. McEwan has expressed himself as a writer who wrestles with belief in fiction, and one of his critics, Sebastian Groes, has argued that McEwan's authorship begins with, and is sustained

3. Groes, (2013), p. 149.

by, an enquiry into himself and the possibilities of fiction. McEwan recently compared himself as a novelist to a Victorian clergyman riddled with doubt, coming to the edge of collapse and thinking 'Did I ever believe?', and not knowing how or when to suspend his disbelief in novels.[4] The reading list Daisy gives her father leads him to conclude that 'the supernatural was the recourse of an insufficient imagination, a dereliction of duty, a childish evasion of the difficulties and wonders of the real, of the demanding re-enactment of the plausible' (67-8). Here McEwan seems to extol the value of literary imagination while belittling the possibility that imagination has a role in theology. McEwan is committed to imagination as the source of fiction, but seems strangely averse to imagination as a source of theology and religious practice. If imagination is sufficient to conjure up characters and their stories that can add value to human experience, is imagination also capable of creating a god-story? As I argued in chapter 1, what is imagined is not unreal, the imagined is no less real than the tangible, and the opposite of that which is tangibly real is not unreality. Rather, the product of imagination may be thought of as being irreal. This means that the imagined has reality, but does not exist in the real world in the way that either an aeroplane, such as Perowne observes, or a brain, on which he operates, does. The imagined is made-up, but is no less real for that. Throughout *Saturday*, McEwan explores faith in fiction – in effect, the made-up imagined world of make-believe – over against religious belief.

On the day when the novel's narrated events take place, protestors march through London to express opposition to the Iraq War. The march hinders Perowne's journey to play squash, and, because of a diversion, he becomes involved in a road traffic accident, after which a violent altercation with the brutish other driver, named Baxter, occurs. Perowne later realises that Baxter's brutishness is the understandable result of believing he has no future, thereby being free of any sense of future accountability for actions in the present (210). Returning from his game of squash, Perowne buys fish for the stew he will make that evening when his family will gather, and he muses about the chances that that particular fish, of all the fish in the sea, would end up in his stew:

> The random ordering of the world, the unimaginable odds against any particular condition, still please him. Even as a child, and especially after Aberfan, he never believed in fate or providence, or the future being made by someone in the

4. *ibid.*, p. 5.

sky. Instead, at every instant, a trillion trillion possible futures; the pickiness of pure chance and physical laws seemed like freedom from the scheming of a gloomy god (128).

McEwan thus puts to the reader questions to do with coincidence and determinism, cause and effect, randomness and intention, that, for Christians, are specifically theological questions.

If, as McEwan suggests, 'the human disposition is to believe. And when proved wrong, shift ground. Or have faith, and go on believing' (151), readers will ask where there is scope for the numinous, mystical or supernatural in the world of *Saturday*. At least two episodes in the novel provide answers. The first occurs after Perowne has visited his mother in a residential home for those living with dementia. Before he begins to prepare for the family's evening together, he visits an old music hall theatre where his son, Theo, plays guitar in a band. He lets the music – edgy saxophone, bass guitar and driving rhythm – engulf him. In a passage reminiscent of the transformative concert hall scene in E.M. Forster's *Howards End*, McEwan writes,

> There are these rare moments when musicians together touch something sweeter than they've ever found before in rehearsals or performance. . . . This is when they give us a glimpse of what we might be, of our best selves, and of an impossible world in which you give everything you have to others, but lose nothing of yourself (171).

This phraseology is Gospel language, referring back to the idealistic, and probably unattainable, absolutist ethics of Christ's Sermon on the Mount. McEwan, indeed, makes more specific reference to this otherworldly dream when he writes of 'Christ's Kingdom on earth, the workers' paradise, the ideal Islamic state' (172). These religious and political dreams, he suggests, are beyond us, for 'only in music, and only on rare occasions, does the curtain actually lift on this dream of community, and it's tantalisingly conjured, before fading away with the last notes' (172). Later, readers find McEwan showing that this is not unique to music, for the second episode hinting at the power of the numinous comes at the novel's denouement. This hinges on a highly improbable *deus ex machina* when Daisy recites Matthew Arnold's poem 'Dover Beach' so effectively that it melts the heart of one of the intruders holding Perowne's family hostage. While this may be seen as demonstrating the liberating and transformative potential of art, I suspect that McEwan, despite his wavering faith in fiction, is suggesting that Baxter's recognition of the existence, personhood and value of another human, probably for the first time in his life, brings him to his senses more than any sense of numinosity. Bradley and Tate share this view on the basis that in 'Dover Beach' abandoned faith in organised religion is replaced by what they call 'the private religion' of human relationships in which lovers are true to one another.[5] It is the power of human relationships that wins Baxter over. Nevertheless, the presence of these mystical events is sufficient for the novel to challenge and question the extent to which scientific materialism is capable of offering a satisfactory understanding of the world. There is more to life than meets the eye.

McEwan's choice of 'Dover Beach' for this denouement suits a novel that, as Groes said, is saturated with Mathew Arnold, in particular in their shared interest in the changing relationship between science and religion, the importance and challenges of democracy, tensions within the English class system, and the nature of culture and society. These have become themes of intense significance in the early years of the twenty-first century, warning us of the dangers of the democratisation of religion and the distancing of some sections of society from religious institutions. Even though McEwan is known to hold no belief in the supernatural, this is far from being an atheistic novel, and it leaves me pondering a question about the nature of belief: must I believe in the *reality* of God to be a believer? Is it enough to be able to imagine God?

In the novel's final pages, when McEwan flashes hurriedly forward through the years immediately after Perowne's 'day off, his valuable Saturday' (258), McEwan warns us: 'Beware the utopianists, zealous men certain of the path to the ideal social order' (276-7). Ultimately, McEwan's novel expresses the hope that certainties will transmute into dialogue and debating points. As Perowne prepares for bed at the end of Saturday thinking 'faintly, falling: this day's over', his last thought is 'there's only this' (279). In this final example of intertextuality in a novel full of intertexts, this intentionally echoes the ending of Joyce's story 'The Dead' in *Dubliners* (1914) in which a deathly shroud of snow falls over the city, over both the living and the dead. The pall that falls over Perowne at the end of the day is the pall of sleep, the restorative human condition that deals with memory by relocating events in dreams. Earlier, in Perowne's mother's dementia, McEwan had portrayed the loss of memory as the worst human nightmare, for, as Dominic Head suggests the de-narrated self is a dehumanised self.[6] The

5. *op. cit.*, p. 32.
6. Head, (2007), p. 16.

re-narration, reordering and management of memory is, of course, what religion claims to do. In the case of Christianity, the frequent and regular rehearsal of the Christian narrative in the liturgical recital of creeds and the celebration of the Eucharist gives practitioners a remembered space to locate themselves and their own stories within the bigger story. McEwan seems not to accept that, as in *Saturday*, as in other single-day novels such as *Ulysses* and *Mrs Dalloway*, where, in Laura Marcus's words, 'remembered events pull the present back into the past'[7], religious faith can achieve the same with similar therapeutic effect. McEwan is at the forefront of today's literary search for new values, and religion reserves its place in this quest.

McEwan's critique of religion's conservative, often rebarbative, values becomes more acute in *The Children Act* (2014). The main character is a 59-year-old High Court judge, Fiona Maye, who is trapped in a jaded marriage to a husband yearning for an affair with a younger woman. McEwan is interested not only in how their relationship works out in these circumstances, but also in how Fiona carries out the responsibilities of her profession when reaching conclusions in cases complicated by either religious belief or theological dogma. The novel is, in effect, an atheist's account of an encounter between the secular spirit of the law and religious belief. In the first chapter, Fiona thinks back over some cases she has heard, and their common theme is that at their heart is a religious dilemma. In his accounts of these cases, McEwan's own atheism pulls no punches. One had concerned a strict Chareidi father from Morocco who wanted to remove his daughter from the care of her English mother; another had ruled on the capacity of an Orthodox Jewish father to restrict the educational opportunities his wife wanted for their daughters; and a third intervened in a medical dilemma when the Catholic parents of conjoined twins felt compelled to watch both their children die, although the medical profession had argued for saving the life of one child at the expense of the other's. In the latter case, the Roman Catholic Archbishop of Westminster had submitted a letter expressing what Fiona felt was a hardline view, that he would prefer to see no medical intervention so that God's will for the children was not frustrated (29). Stated as baldly as this, his view seems harsh, but Fiona is neither surprised nor concerned that churchmen would prefer to hold a theological line rather than make compromises for 'pastoral' reasons. Fiona's role, as a judge, is to negotiate the rapids between the Scylla and Charybdis of medical and religious principles.

7. In Groes, *op. cit.*, p. 96.

The case Fiona has now taken on is an emergency hearing in which a hospital is challenging the right of a seventeen-year-old Jehovah's Witness with leukaemia, named Adam, to refuse a blood transfusion. Without this he would face 'a horrible [and certain] death' (67). Among the legal arguments Fiona hears are several provocative points about the nature of Adam's religion and his beliefs about God.

First, the consultant states that Adam's refusal of treatment is 'based on the doctrines of a religious cult for which he may well become a pointless martyr' (68). The barrister representing Adam's supportive parents points out that 'cult' is a strong word, then asks whether the consultant has any religious belief. On answering that he was an Anglican, the barrister asks whether the Church of England is a cult. Atheists – including atheist novelists – might think so. Christian readers might ask whether any religion can be described as a cult, and, if so, what are the characterising features of a cult?

Second, the legal argument for refusing blood transfusion and the theological basis for the Witnesses' ban on transfusion revolve around the interpretation of a biblical injunction against eating blood. Adam's father refers to Genesis, Leviticus and Acts, and argues that the Hebrew translated as 'eat' means 'take into the body' (78). On this basis, transfusion is forbidden. In relation to this legal point, Christian readers might ask how we ensure proper or appropriate interpretations of the Bible. How do we derive ethical guidance on modern dilemmas from an ancient text? A Jehovah's Witness informs Fiona that 'The Governing Body is Jehovah's channel of communication to us. It's his voice. If there are changes in the teaching it's because God only gradually reveals his purpose' (80-1). When a governing religious body colludes with harmful interpretation and acts as guardian of the sacred text, what can be done?

Moving from the courtroom to the hospital ward, where Fiona visits Adam to ascertain whether he is mature enough to know his own mind, legal arguments continue both in her own mind and in the conversation she has with Adam. One is to do with the nature of religion as a group delusion. She accepts Adam's point that if, in a court of law, several people who had never spoken to each other all offered the same account of an event, then their account is more likely to be true, but she qualifies her agreement with him because 'people who don't know each other can be gripped by the same false idea' (100-1). In support, she cites a case when the authorities falsely accused parents of satanic abuse of children. Might all Adam's fellow Jehovah's Witnesses be similarly deluded by their own wishful thinking? Is religious faith a form of group delusion? And, how might religious believers rebut that charge?

Fiona oversteps the legal mark when she discusses with Adam the implications on his physical wellbeing and life expectancy if he does not receive blood, and asks, 'Would it please God, to have you blind or stupid or on dialysis for the rest of your life?' (105). He is disgruntled that she is discussing what will, or will not, please God when she may not believe in God at all (106), but admits that he would hate it if his illness were to worsen. Nevertheless, he would have to accept it. Christian readers, who are unlikely to share Adam's stance in medical ethics, will ask similar questions as they read this section of the novel and arrive at quite different answers to those Adam offers. He shares with Fiona a poem he has written, inspired by a comment made by one of the congregation elders, who remarked that if the worst were to happen to Adam it would fill the church with love. Fiona sums up the thrust of the poem as 'Satan comes to beat you with his hammer, and without meaning to he flattens your soul into a sheet of gold that reflects God's love on everyone and for this you are saved and it doesn't matter so much that you are dead' (109). Adam's parents believe that 'God had visited leukaemia on [their] son' (74), but many contemporary mainstream Christians will be most uncomfortable with this appalling cruelty. Nevertheless, the novel leaves us asking how we account for the presence of debilitating illness and premature death in a world created by a supposedly good God.

At the conclusion of all arguments, Fiona finds that Adam is mature enough to know his own mind, but argues that he must be protected from his religion. He, his parents and his church have made a decision that is hostile to his welfare. For this reason, and because his life is more precious than his dignity, she orders the transfusion to take place. This leads us to ask: when might religion be harmful, and when might people need protecting from their religious beliefs?

After Adam receives blood he writes to Fiona and describes the joy he and his parents felt (138). Later, however, he confides in Fiona that he had felt pure and good, noble and heroic as he refused treatment, but now he is confused. She suggests he has lost his faith, but he fears admitting this out loud. Nevertheless, he finds himself saying, 'Once you take a step back from the Witnesses, you might as well go all the way' (165). His ensuing question could be that of a twenty-first-century New Atheist or, indeed, of one who sees a positive role for the make-believe of fiction in theology: 'Why replace one tooth fairy with another?' (165). I have heard no reports of tooth fairies causing people harm, and they perhaps serve some purpose for children distressed by the loss of milk teeth: is there anything wrong, therefore, in religious stories that help people to take stock of what happens to them in life? The tooth fairy image, even if Adam intended it to do so, may not entirely negate all aspects of religion.

Among literary texts, novels are noted for being layered texts. *The Children Act*, although not much more than novella length, has many layers: the legal profession and its methods, Fiona and Jack's marriage, Adam's growing maturity that includes journeys in and out of religious belief, the tortuous complexities of medical ethics in the twenty-first-century world, the nature of cultic religion and its theological code. These layers, rather than laid on each other like strata, wrap around each other like an onion. Peel away the papery dustjacket and the underlying layers, and what lies at the core? I contend that what lies at the core of *The Children Act* is, to use Salman Rushdie's words, the question of a quarrel with God.

Rushdie is famed for intricate multi-layered novels. Set in a Muslim world, an Arabic history and a Middle Eastern tradition of storytelling, *The Enchantress of Florence* (2009) sets out the infinite possibility of fiction to imagine any world and any era, in which, if we are ready to suspend disbelief, the notion of God can be created or uncreated. In the make-believe of fiction, authors can persuade readers to imagine theistic worlds. Bradley and Tate describe the novel as 'characteristically exuberant, historically mischievous and theologically demanding'.[8] In addition, I find it exuberantly bawdy at times. Almost all of Rushdie's novels enjoy interplay between the mystical and the mundane, and readers can never be sure whether what he describes in his novels belongs to the realm of the actual or the impossible. As if longing for a world where 'the visionary revelatory dream-poetry of the quotidian [has] not yet been crushed by blinkered, prosy fact' (12), Rushdie's novels play with the poetry of the magical and the prose of actuality. *The Enchantress of Florence* mixes dense, well-researched history (not many novels have a bibliography as lengthy as this has), magical realism and allegory. Its main character, Emperor Akbar, based on the actual seventeenth-century Mughal, who believed in the value of all religions, is exhausted by a crisis of faith that ends with his suspicion that, despite his efforts to the contrary, the world will be a place where people 'hate their neighbours and smash their places of worship and kill one another once again in the renewed heat of the great quarrel he had sought to end for ever, the quarrel over God' (347). In the lecture entitled 'Is Nothing Sacred?', read by Harold Pinter on Rushdie's behalf in 1990 when he was in hiding because of the *fatwa* set against him in 1989,

8. *ibid.*, p. 82.

Rushdie expressed desire that novels might give room both for religions to quarrel and for questions about God to be explored, without breaking out in violence. He has Akbar repeat this hope in *The Enchantress of Florence* when first acceding to the throne. Akbar longs for a time and a place where 'everything could be said to everyone by anyone on any subject, including the non-existence of God and the abolition of kings' (45). 'In the house of God,' he says, 'all voices are free to speak as they choose, and that is the form of their devotion' (44).

The religious world of *The Enchantress of Florence* is plural – Hindu, Muslim and Christian. The author creating this world is an atheist of Muslim descent. He plays with the power of story to create both artifice and belief. One of Akbar's first decisions as Emperor is to establish a temple, which he calls the Tent of the New Worship. This revolutionary building was to be an impermanent location where argument was to be the only god, for reason is a mortal divinity (98). Flimsy, easily torn and perishable canvas, with which the temple was constructed, 'well represented the impermanence of the things of the mind' (99), for it implies the flimsy substance of faith. In this Tent of the New Worship the fundamental question worshippers face is whether there is a true religion other than an 'eternal handing down' (102). Why should anyone hold on to a faith simply because it was believed by our fathers and their fathers? Has religious faith been reduced to family habit? Disturbingly, Akbar's guest, Mogor Dell'Amore, describes the new temple as 'a hall of mirrors, full of illusions and inversions' (99). Akbar is appalled at the audacity of his guest, yet the charge still stands: is all that is reflected in that place of worship merely a distortion of truth? Akbar notes that the Winemen and the Waterers, the two main groupings of worshippers in the Tent, call one another heretics and fools, and he wants to sweep the whole argument aside: 'If man had created god then man could uncreate him too. . . . Could a god, once created, become impossible to destroy?' (103). This seems to be the religious question at the core of this novel. Rushdie's own answer to the question is related to our understanding of the nature of fiction. After a character named Nino Argalia tells a short tale of a Partly-dead Giant, the narrator remarks, 'The story was completely untrue, but the untruth of untrue stories could sometimes be of service in the real world' (211). Rushdie tells stories because they are like the 'house of adoration', the hall of mirrors, the Tent of the New Worship that Akbar built: they can host gods and take diverse forms of faith seriously. For this reason, and perhaps because Christian theology should be open to the possibility that God is a human construct, *The*

Enchantress of Florence is, for me, not an ungodly novel. Rushdie, a 'Muslim atheist', does not write books against God, but books that invite us to imagine God.

The protagonist in James Wood's debut novel of 2004, on the other hand, *is* writing a book against God. That the novel takes *The Book against God* as its title provokes readers to assess whether or not the novel is indeed anti-theist. In my view, the novel is more a lament for a lost world, a lost Eden, an orchard blighted by the presence of a worm, than an argument for either the non-existence or the malevolence of God, for the book ends with Thomas Bunting looking back on a generally happy childhood while asking why there was a worm in it.

Bradley and Tate's critical introduction to post-9/11 atheist novels assumes that most anglophone novels, haunted by faith, are engaged in a self-conscious struggle with their biblical heritage. If this is so, *The Book against God* demonstrates this not only in the symbolism of its principal characters' names – the doubting son Thomas is pitted against his more faithful father Peter, a vicar and rock of the Church – but also in frequent references to the book of Psalms, as well as in the possibility that the entire novel is a retelling of Jesus's parable of the prodigal son.

Thomas is a putative obituarist who studiously avoids writing obituaries, a lackadaisical doctoral student perpetually delaying submitting his thesis, an habitual liar and a collector of atheist sayings that he records in his commonplace book against God. This, he says, is his main project. Wood presents him as a hopeless case: he is unable to carry a tune, his apartment is dishevelled and he lies endlessly to fend off people chasing him for the repayment of debts. Feckless, he is, above all else, a failed husband, separated from his wife, Jane, since the September before his father died. His friend Max suggests that Thomas's atheist project is a covert prayer to God, whom he believes is its intended reader, and that Thomas is haunted by the faith he desperately tries to disprove. He is, like many atheist novelists, an atheist who cannot stop talking about God. Thomas had spent the Christmas before his father died in his childhood home. While there, he crept away to his room on the pretext of working on his thesis. Instead he read 'one of those religious apologists who get [him] so angry'. What angers him in particular is the arbitrary and conventional manner in which they switch their discussion of the presence of suffering in the world to a depiction of Christ on the cross. Their description of a world of meaningless suffering has been, to use his term, correct, but, in his view, those who belittle the sense of meaninglessness in suffering when they attribute meaning, even love, to the suffering endured at Christ's crucifixion. As he reads, he rejects the cross and, in ghostly faith, he makes a cross of his fingers at the cross, like a potential victim warding off a vampire (173-4). Later, he philosophises and wonders which would be more pleasant to live in – a free world where there is suffering or a painless, unfree world. He believes it is not his task to choose between these, but to 'imagine such a world, and *just by imagining* it to prove that the world we currently live in did not need to be made the way it was made. If [he] could imagine such a world, how much greater might God's imagining of it have been?' (179). His ability to imagine alternative worlds and alternative futures, especially suffering-free worlds, is an expression of a religious hope retained from his childhood in a Christian home. In this respect, if in no other, Thomas Bunting is like his author: Wood, too, is the son of a clergyman and no longer holds his father's faith. He has moved from the country of his birth to the United States, and from a home where Christianity was practised to an atheistic position. As literary criticism representative on the board of the International Society for Heresy Studies, Wood is interested in seeking greater understanding of heresy, blasphemy and unbelief in literature. He uses his novels as part of this venture.

The sermon towards the end of *The Book against God*, a eulogy Thomas gives at his father's funeral, although aborted partway through at his wife's insistence, provides opportunity for a contrast between Thomas and Peter. They had not agreed about everything and were fundamentally opposed on many points, with Thomas describing himself as a theological philosopher and Peter as a philosophical theologian. This philosophical theology was symbolised in the sticker Peter had attached to the cover of his Bible. It read, 'This is an advance copy sent in lieu of a proof', which Thomas interpreted both as a hint of complicating anxiety and a sign of sophisticated belief (230). He remarked that he had entered a life of devotion to God and vocation to the priesthood in order to find the faith he had lost in the theology faculty (215). As a priest in a County Durham parish he was socially elevated, but as result of 'his gentle, undogmatic faith, he fitted himself around the lives of his flock' (57). According to Thomas, they had rarely talked about their differences, partly because, as a former lecturer in theology, Peter had 'aerated his theology with so many little holes, so much flexibility and doubt and easy-going tolerance, that he simply disappeared down one of these holes' (46). He had immense capacity for evasion in arguments. In the eulogy at his father's funeral, Thomas expresses his belief that life is 'a bowl of tears', in which the degrees to which people suffer vary. Like all others, Peter had suffered, 'but he used to joke that he was absurdly happy . . . and was seeking for the key of *un*happiness' (233). Repeated expressions of unbelief in the eulogy unsettle the mourners and climax in Thomas's assertion that Peter was no angel. At this point, Jane and Canon Palliser bring Thomas to a halt, later expressing the view that he was overwrought and rambling (234).

In the course of the novel, Thomas presents several arguments against God. The first that drives Thomas away from unquestioning belief is the presence of pain. This came upon him when he heard his father in church lead prayers of intercession that listed difficulties people were experiencing in life. He heard these as if they were pages of atrocious international news or tragic local news ripped from daily newspapers. At first he thought such atrocities 'vandalised the very face of God', but soon realised that his father saw them as events in 'God's world [which had been] vandalised by man' (52). This takes him into an interiorised discussion in which he rejects the notion that pain is present because we need to be corrected by God. Rather, it seems that God has created a flawed world and abandoned us in it, and 'The most charitable image of this particular God he can produce is that of a father who breaks his own son's leg just so that he can watch his son learn how to appeal to his dad for help in mending it' (52). Later he describes religion as a scab remaining after an injury, always there as a constant reminder of previous pain (106). How can Christian believers rebut this charge?

The second argument is related to the nature of humanity. Whenever Thomas visited his parents, he habitually went to evensong at the cathedral. He was equally horrified and amused at choir boys singing words of 'ungraspable maturity' from the Book of Common Prayer (121). Boys, who kicked a football around in the schoolyard without a care in the world, sang, 'Have mercy upon us, have mercy upon us, for we are utterly despised' (122). In the narrator's voice, Thomas asks,

> Are we utterly despised? I don't feel at all despised. Do we need to beg for mercy? But what sins have those little boys committed? Whose hearts are unclean? Not mine, certainly not my late father's parishioners. . . . Now, I ask you, what sins have these people committed? What sins? They kneel and intone their confessions . . . but what has any of them done in the week since last Sunday's cringing absolution? (122)

This leads to what he calls a 'strange thought', which, if they did not believe in this God, they would not need to prostrate and humiliate themselves pleading for forgiveness. He was thirteen, and the thought liberated him. He learnt that, whether or not he believed God existed, he still left church unharmed, ate lunch and watched the rain, which falls on the just and unjust alike, fall in the garden (122-3). We might ask ourselves whether this version of the doctrine of human nature stands up to examination. Must we demean ourselves before God when we gather for worship? Does the Cranmerian language – 'there is no health in us' – overstate the sin we carry? What would be the appropriate form of confession in contemporary church services? The problem Thomas seems to pose for modern Christian readers is whether a human race less conscious of oppressive sinfulness needs God in the same way. This brings us to the novel's third objection to the real existence of God, which is that God is a human construct.

The novel twice expresses this notion in the form of a positive statement about religion's contribution to the human condition. First, Max suggests that 'since religion is a human creation, and its form is man's then . . . everything in it is at least as true as we are' (106), and, later, Thomas remembers this as 'if religion has the form of the human, and is the product of humans, it can't be wrong' (165). The logic here is that humanly constructed religions are constructed in such a way that they both encapsulate the prevailing worldview and serve the needs of humanity, but the logic overlooks the possibility that in some circumstances both the worldview and those human needs may be corrupted and ill-meant. In such cases, the humanly constructed religion lacks truth and is wrong. Religion, even as a human construct, must be tested for integrity, authenticity and truth. Humanly constructed religion can often be found to be truth-bearing.

Thomas has a conversation with one of his father's ex-colleagues, Timothy Biffen, who, in the theology department, enjoys the distinction of being a secularist surrounded by believers. Peter never feels sure whether Timothy believes in God. When Thomas attempts to pin him down on this matter, Timothy responds,

> The extremity with which you pose the question – either/or, yes or no, for or against – assumes that one can *know*, that one either believes or doesn't because of some certainty, a certainty founded on inner knowledge – i.e. faith – or some kind of external suggestion, i.e. some kind of vision or visitation, a miracle, or what as you know were in the medieval disposition called 'proofs' of God (161-2).

Can we ever know for sure? Certitude and certainty, it seems to me, have little part to play in the realm of theology and religion where belief is a matter of faith not knowledge. What Rushdie called 'the quarrel over God' is in Wood's novel 'the argumentative wrestle over God' in which the athlete of reason engages with the knight of faith (166). When, shortly before Thomas's birth, Peter had faced his fear about becoming a father, he had entertained doubts about evil, justice and original sin, and tried to imagine a world without God. Taking God out of the world, he realised, did not make the world any less horrid, but made it even more horrid, for any hope of salvation or succour had also been removed. Furthermore, he realised that we do not know why evil exists, but believed it had been created along with everything else for a reason. He concluded, at least to his own satisfaction, that because he would rather be alive than dead, even if the world is full of pain, that there must be more love in the world than there is pain (217). Readers must take such arguments within the novel's dialogues and consider whether they stand or fall according to our own experience of life and faith.

In his essays on literature and belief, Wood argued that 'fiction moves in the *shadow of doubt*, knows itself to be a true lie, knows that at any point it might fail to make its case'.[9] If he sees *The Book against God* as moving in the shadow of doubt, the possibility of God may be left open. The novel may tell an untrue story impregnated with untruths that may yet be of value to human society. Moreover, it permits a Christian reading of a supposedly atheist novel. In its constant wrangle over belief, unbelief and the irrepressible urge to avoid unbelief, the novel nimbly avoids the fate of the chameleon that exploded when it sat on a tartan rug (79).

Atheist fiction stimulates creative and rigorous Christian apologetics in that it makes readers who believe in God examine their beliefs and test their capacity to resist challenge. Open-minded and free-thinking Christian readers will not be upset by any of the religiosity, spirituality or atheology in any of the books discussed in this chapter. Rather, they will be taken into new and verdant avenues of creative thinking, each of which has the potential of enhancing faith, deepening spirituality and enriching one's apprehension of divinity. Atheism carries the misfortune of being defined by what it is not. It is a negation of belief, and an atheist is someone who is not a theist. There are, of course, more positive ways to describe the atheistic stance, such as 'secularist' or 'humanist'. Such terms countermand the extremist theist view that atheism is necessarily immoral or amoral, for the principles of secularism and humanism guide ethical behaviour as effectively as theistic belief. We do not need a higher being to make us moral beings. Being moral – knowing what is right and

9. Wood, (1999), pp. xiv-xv.

good – is simply part of what it means to be fully human. We are *homo moralis*, with an innate capacity to behave with dignity in virtuous and humane ways. One of Virginia Woolf's characters, Clarissa Dalloway, described her 'atheistic religion' as 'doing good for the sake of goodness' (87). Surely being good because one wants to be good, morality born of desire, is a higher morality than that born out of obedience.

Atheist novelists are not only seeking transcendence in secular form, but may also be challenging the notion of the sacred, the practice of religion, the hypocrisy of some believers and what they see as the folly and inconsistencies of theology. At this point, the question that underpins *Make-Believe* becomes most acute: why, in a less religious age, do novelists persist in exploring religious, theological and spiritual themes? In the case of atheist novels, the answer may simply be that they cannot avoid talking about God. In their quests for grandeur in this world, for transcendence away from sacredness, and for a sense of Otherness that is not recognisably the God of orthodox religion, they cannot but become garrulous about religion and theology. The quarrel over God is their inescapable subject, and religious readers can readily get their teeth into that.

Chapter 8

BIBLE-INSPIRED FICTION

At the turn of the twenty-first century, cleverly targeted marketing saved Anita Diamant's *The Red Tent* from being almost forgotten. So many hardback copies remained unsold that, in advance of a proposed paperback edition, the publishers sent free copies of the hardback to female rabbis, Christian clergy and the leaders of women's reading groups. Within four years, by 2001, this previously ignored book had become a best seller. It thus encapsulates three stages of change in the contemporary world of publishing: the 'if you enjoyed that you will like this' style of targeted marketing that has become a standard feature of online bookselling, the reading group phenomenon that restores both the social aspect of reading and the role of 'word of mouth' recommendation, and what might be regarded as the surprising rediscovery of biblical narrative as a source of fiction. *The Red Tent* retells the story of Dinah's rape that, in Genesis 34, interrupts the Jacob narrative. The genre of what we can call biblical fictions seems strange in a secular age, yet the early years of the twenty-first century have witnessed a tidal wave of such novels. If fewer are reading the Bible, why would people choose to read fictionalised accounts of Bible stories?

Of course, from the early years of novel writing, biblical stories have been sources for novels. Biblical sources can be found in Defoe's *The Life and Adventures of Robinson Crusoe*, first published in 1719 and widely regarded as the first English novel, although it also has origins in the real-life adventures of the ship-wrecked castaway Alexander Selkirk, and its style was inspired by the spiritual life writing of Augustine's *Confessions* and John Bunyan's *Grace Abounding*. The novel has often been read as a rewriting and interpretation of the story of Jonah, referenced early in the novel when a ship's captain urged Crusoe never to go to sea again after his first ominously disastrous voyage: 'Perhaps this has all befallen us on your account, like Jonah in the ship of Tarshish' (13). On this voyage,

Crusoe, like Jonah, had cowered in his cabin while the storm raged and had only come up on deck to help at the pumps when he saw the crew at their prayers. Jonah's essential loneliness – on board the ship, in the belly of the great fish, on vigil outside Nineveh and set apart from the rest of humanity as God's chosen spokesperson – sets the tone for Crusoe's condition later in Defoe's novel. Defoe almost always refers to the island in terms of a desert or a wilderness and often has Crusoe fretting about why he is singled out for special trials. For instance, Crusoe marvels at the way corn grows in the vicinity of his hut to such an extent that he is moved to give thanks to God for what seems as miraculous as the gourd that grew to shelter Jonah, but, in contrast, his first attempts to sow corn fail and the harvest is as withered as Jonah's gourd eventually is. In these and other ways, Defoe's novel uses the Jonah narrative as a foundation story to face readers with ultimate questions about self-perception and the nature of reality: to what extent is human existence a lonely struggle against the elements in a wild place? Furthermore, the Bible itself uses the Jonah story as a fiction to question the scope of God's mission and concern.

An early English novel with an explicit use of biblical narrative as a source, more so than Defoe's, is Henry Fielding's *Joseph Andrews*, first published in 1742. While it lampoons characters Fielding borrowed from Samuel Richardson and uses their comic escapades to examine critically some aspects of contemporary society, its shape and eponymous hero come from the character and adventures of the biblical Joseph, son of Isaac. In his second letter to Pamela, Joseph Andrews describes himself as the biblical Joseph's namesake and declares that, like him, he seeks to maintain his 'virtue against all temptations' (41). Robbers ambush both Josephs; both Josephs face an ultimate showdown, one in the Pharaoh's court, the other in Squire Boothby's country seat; and both Josephs are finally reconciled with people they left behind through revelations of identity. The biblical Joseph was initially unrecognised by his brothers who came to Egypt to do trade, and Joseph Andrews discovered that his parents are not who he thought they were and that Pamela is not his sister.[1] On reading the adventures of Joseph Andrews and his companion Abraham Adams, we discover that, while Fielding claimed to be writing an epic (1), he in fact writes in *three* epic traditions: the Homeric epic he cites in the preface, the travel epic he alludes to in his longer title that ends 'Written in Imitation of Cervantes, Author of Don Quixote', and the biblical epic of the patriarchal narratives.

---

1. Harold Fisch exhaustively traces the web of biblical allusions in *Joseph Andrews* in his *New Stories for Old*. The scope of this chapter permits no more than hints at the parallels.

Making these comments about Defoe and Fielding is saying nothing new, and the tradition of novels based on biblical stories has continued in the intervening centuries. However, in the case of the contemporary phenomenon of biblical fictions, the protagonists are biblical personae fictionalised, whereas in the earlier novels, Crusoe is only *based* on Jonah and Joseph Andrews is clearly none other than Joseph the patriarch. Some writers such as David Maine and Jenny Diski have majored on retelling Old Testament stories, with Maine publishing novels retelling the stories of the Fall, Noah's flood and Samson, and Diski publishing two novels, the first based on the Abraham narrative and the second on the next generation in the patriarchal narratives. Significant Old Testament women such as Esther and Eve have also attracted the attention of several writers of biblical fiction.[2]

The New Testament has brought novelists to its pages for source material, too. Writers such as C.K. Stead, Simon Mawer and Michael Dickinson have to some extent been inspired by the discovery of *The Gospel of Judas* in the 1970s, which was eventually published in the early years of the twenty-first century, and chose to write novels focused on Judas's story, one of Christ's most fascinating disciples.[3] Their precursors included medieval texts such as *The Golden Legend* of circa 1260, whose author, Jacobus, drew on apocryphal material to provide a murderous backstory for his arch-villain, and Jorge Luis Borges's short story, 'Three Versions of Judas', published in 1944 in *Ficciones*. The academic at the centre of Borges's story responds to adverse reactions to his efforts to account for Judas's actions by rewriting the story three times, until he ends up with what he calls a 'monstrous' version. They also stand in the tradition of pietistic novels imagining the lives of Jesus's disciples such as Lloyd C. Douglas's *The Big Fisherman* of 1949, yet Dickinson's, Mawer's and Stead's versions of the story of Judas are more scandalous. Dickinson's novel, *The Lost Testament of Judas Iscariot* (1994), purports to be the text of an apologia addressed by Judas to Peter in which Judas exposes the intrigue he was involved in. Dickinson's Judas had begged Jesus not to go through with his face-off with the religious and political authorities in Jerusalem, and then conspired with Darius, another follower of Jesus, to save Jesus from his fate. Darius agreed to stand in for Jesus, and, although Jesus insisted that Judas should inform the authorities that the wrong man has been handed over, Darius dies on

2. Eve has attracted much attention from authors such as Lamming, Aidenhoff and Elliott, while Kohn's retelling of Esther stands almost alone.
3. In Brendan Kennelly's prize-winning book-length poem *The Little Book of Judas*, Judas remarks, 'All kinds of scribblers find me an absorbing theme.'

the cross, too far away from onlookers to be recognised. When, after Darius's hasty burial, Judas persuades Jesus that he can now fake his resurrection, Jesus says he never wants to see Judas's face again. Having watched the women discover the empty tomb and meet Jesus, Judas does not know what to do or where to go, so he seeks help from Martha who, for Jesus's sake, gives him sanctuary in the tomb. There Judas is trapped because Peter does not come as expected, and his apologia comes to an abrupt end as the light disappears, and his life ends slowly as the air is consumed. This is a clever rewriting of the events of Holy Week, and it is interesting to speculate how destructive it would be of Christianity if Dickinson's version were historically true.

Mawer's novel *The Gospel of Judas* (2000), written before the contents of the *Gospel of Judas* were in the public domain, interweaves four related narratives. The first is that of a scholarly priest, Leo, working on an ancient codex in which Judas claims to have seen the decomposing body of Jesus; the second is the Judas story behind the codex; the third is that of the older Leo now defrocked; and the fourth is the story of Leo's mother's tragic love affair in wartime Rome. These independent but related narratives are brought together by the unifying themes of betrayal and resurrection. Stead's novel *My Name was Judas* (2006) was published only shortly after Dickinson's and Mawer's, but after a great awakening in Judas studies had occurred because it came after Judas's Gospel had become common knowledge. His novel imagines a decent and fair-minded Judas, now an old man retired from his work as a trader, looking back on his childhood and youth and setting down, in poetry and prose, for the sake of his children, an account of how he came to be unjustly reviled as a traitor. Such books about Judas might trouble some Christian believers: some will worry that they fly in the face of aspects of biblical evidence including the Gospel's clear suggestion that Judas did not live to be an old man, and others will fret about the role of Judas in Jesus's last days, but this seems to me to be the point of these novels. The role of Judas as given in the New Testament is itself troubling: what sort of God predestines someone to adopt the role of traitor and consign him to an awful death, and what if Judas had taken a different course of action? These novels encourage thoughtful exploration of these issues.

Fictionalised accounts of the story of Jesus form another subgroup within the genre of biblical fiction. It is certainly not a recent phenomenon: George Moore's *The Brook Kerith*, published in 1927, presents Jesus as a pre-crucifixion wonder-worker and a post-resurrection shepherd when it depicts Joseph of Arimathea finding Jesus in a coma and nursing him back to health. Some fictionalised accounts of the story of Jesus have caused violence and global protests, such as when Martin Scorsese's 1988 film, *The Last Temptation of Christ*, based on Nikos Kazantzakis's 1955 novel of the same title, was first screened. Controversy about fictionalised Jesuses was most recently revived with the publication of Philip Pullman's *The Good Man Jesus and the Scoundrel Christ* as part of the Canongate Myths Series (which includes other retold Bible stories, David Grossman's *Lion's Honey* about Samson and *The Fire Gospel* by Michel Faber). Pullman's novella follows the general lines of the Synoptic Gospels for the narrative, but adds one radical innovation: the author splits the character of Jesus into two, one a sickly child called Christ who is favoured by his mother, the other a lusty, healthy boy called Jesus. The chief heresy of the novel – that Jesus really does die and his brother, Christ, plays the part of his resurrected person in some sort of publicity stunt – is less authorial mischief than purposeful invention. It is intended to highlight the disjunction between the historical Jesus Christ and the Christian Church, whose behaviour has often not shown love to its neighbours. Sadly, those who are offended by the heresy miss the force of Pullman's satire. Between Moore in 1927 and Pullman in 2010, fictionalised accounts of Jesus's life include some well-known works such as *King Jesus* (1946) by Robert Graves whose abiding interest in myths is so far to the fore in this novel that it is marred by the ease with which readers sense the dangers of Gnosticism and are not convinced by the text; Norman Mailer's *The Gospel According to the Son* (1997) emphasises the humanity of its central character so much that we are reminded of the delicate doctrinal balance in the hypostatic union, and it causes us to think deeply about the humanity and divinity of Christ; and *The Gospel According to Jesus Christ* (1993) by José Saramago, a communist atheist whose satirical intention in the novel is achieved by inverting the moral polarities of the universe. Satan, renamed Pastor in the novel, is on Jesus's side and looks after him. Jesus at the end bewails the mess the world is in as a result of Christianity. I might also mention Nikos Kazantzakis's *The Last Temptation of Christ*, whose novel is not blasphemous as those who protested outside screenings of its film version alleged, but is, rather, a sturdy defence of Christian orthodoxy against the Docetic heresy. In addition, there is Anne Rice's two-volume work, *Christ the Lord: Out of Egypt* (2005) and *Christ the Lord: The Road to Cana* (2008), which are first-person narratives faithful to the New Testament, and whose popularity derives both from the author's previous success as a writer of vampire thrillers and the pietism of conservative American Christian readers, whose company she briefly joined during the years she wrote these quite unimaginative novels. She has since left the church.

Others concentrate on particular episodes of the canonical Jesus's life. Good examples of these include Michèle Roberts's *The Wild Girl* (1984), which takes the form of a fifth Gospel supposedly written by Mary Magdalene giving her account of the relationship she had with Jesus, and Jim Crace's *Quarantine* (1997), which imagines an alternative account of Jesus's forty days in the wilderness. In their various ways, these and other fictionalised accounts of the life of Jesus pose questions about the historicity of the canonical Gospels, the perspective from which the Gospel narratives were written and the adequacy of Christological interpretations. They thus facilitate fresh readings of the Gospels and sharpen our attentiveness to their nuances, largely because appreciation of the art of storytelling draws attention to the techniques the Gospel writers employed, as well as their theological and evangelical intentions.

Three main types of biblical fictions have emerged recently: those that retell the stories to fill their lacunae, amplify their themes or explore the psychology of their characters; those that refocus the stories, telling them from a different perspective; and those that confound the stories by testing, probing, challenging or subverting their assumed norms.

Biblical fictions of the first type belong to, or, more accurately, are derivative of, an honoured rabbinical tradition of Midrash. In Midrash, the primary interpretative tool of a biblical text was playful exploration of a text's gaps, inconsistencies and foibles. The technique fell into disuse by about 700 CE. Often moving far from the text's plain sense, Midrash relied on each word and gap in the text being pregnant with meaning and on all possible lines of interpretation being kept open. Although some elements of Christianity have found Midrash problematic because it resists interpretative finality and contradicts the oft-held opinion that there might be a best (or even correct) interpretation of any text, supplementations of the biblical narratives in the fictions of novelists such as David Maine and Jenny Diski explode this cautious view, and help readers to discover the multiplicity of interpretative layers and wealth of meaning in biblical narrative. In an article in which he expressed concern that the Bible stories are becoming almost forgotten, Maine explained that he retells some of its stories in his novels partly because the original stories suggest so much but tell so little, but also because they ignore the psychology and motivation of the characters that interest many modern readers and he wants to explore these with us. He also noted that the narratives can be changed so much while remaining unchanged, but his most pressing reason for Maine retelling Bible stories is because, so long as readers keep responding to them, writers will keep turning to these stories and he wants to ensure that they are remembered.[4] Evidently, straightforward retellings of this type are capable of drawing out theological and spiritual themes of significance to contemporary readers, as well as giving voice to biblically silent characters like Noah's wife, Isaac as Abraham bound him and Judas at the Last Supper.

When a novelist refocalises a biblical story by reorienting its narratival perspective, readers often find this refreshingly illuminating as new light is cast on the tale, its character and its themes. Authors tell such refocused tales to point away from the original biblical perspective, which is dominating, to foreground a subsumed, hidden or neglected facet of the narrative. To demonstrate the technique, you might look at John Millais's painting *The Boyhood of Raleigh*, completed in 1870, where two boys are enthralled by a tale told by an old sailor. Their eyes are fixed on him; he looks at them; he points out to sea; but the onlooker's gaze is drawn, not to where the figures in the painting are focused, but to something to which the older man points, outside both the frame of the painting and his tale. Similarly, biblical fictions often direct readers' attention to characters in the biblical narrative that do not occupy centre ground. For instance, Roberts's *The Wild Girl* focuses its reader's gaze, away from the canonical Gospels' attention on the figure of Jesus, to the story of Mary Magdalene. Not surprisingly given the patriarchal nature of the biblical text, stories refocused on women are particularly common, with several recovering Eve from the strongly implied slur on her character in Genesis,[5] some rescuing neglected and ill-treated biblical women from perpetual victimhood,[6] some (like the short stories of Norma Rosen who identifies herself as a modern Midrashist) exploring how women in the Bible's stories might have reacted to the behaviour of their menfolk,[7] and others lauding the lives and achievements of the Bible's great women, among whom Deborah, Jael, Esther and Judith rank. Some novels based on the story of King David focus readers' interest on his sexuality and relationship with Jonathan, an interesting example of which is Alan Massie's *King David* (1995), whose first sentence – 'Because I am cold and shiver at night, they have procured for me this young girl, Abishag, a Shumanite, that she may share my bed and bring me warmth' (3) – indicates that history has a male gaze, the implication being that Massie's account

---

4. From www.jewishbookweek.com/2007/270207d.php. Accessed 25 June 2012.
5. For instance, Lamming, Elliott and Aidenhoff.
6. For example, Jacobson, *The Rape of Tamar*.
7. *Unbinding Sarah* ponders how Sarah might have reacted to the news of the near-fatal episode when Abraham took his son into the desert.

will liberate the story from men's controlling grasp. Another authorial refocusing technique introduces a sense of timelessness to the novel, often bringing the narrative from times long ago into the present age. For instance, in *The Rape of Tamar* (1970), Dan Jacobson makes the story timeless by having his omniscient first-person narrator make frequent anachronistic references to Jesuitical casuistry and Kantian philosophy, by his use of 'Christ' as an expletive, knowingly referring to an era that has not yet come, and by directly addressing his reader, whom he assumes knows his story. The story does not belong exclusively in the past, but its events could be unfolding as the reader progresses through the text. Its narrative is set free from the shackles of the past.

We live in, and read our novels, in an age suspicious of authoritative texts and showing less respect for dominant religious texts. It is hardly surprising, then, that the third type of biblical fiction comprises novels that in some way confound the biblical narratives. These set out to undermine the theological or historical truth of the original story, and they abound. Consider the story of Noah with its troubling portrayal of a God who makes mistakes, who reverses decisions, who is ready to exterminate the human race like vermin and who needs to be reminded not to do the same again. Of the many novelists who have written fictionalised accounts of Noah, the best known are Julian Barnes in *A History of the World in 10½ Chapters* (1989), Michèle Roberts in *The Book of Mrs Noah* (1999), Geraldine McCaughrean in a daring 2004 Whitbread prize-winning children's novel, *Not the End of the World*, Jeanette Winterson in her self-confessedly lame *Boating for Beginners* (1985) and David Maine in *The Flood* (2004). The overall result of such novelistic interest in the Noah saga is, as the last of the aforementioned novels concludes: 'a story like that won't be forgotten. But things will get added and left out and confused, until in a little while people won't even know what's true and what's been made up. The least we can do . . . is get as much of it right as we can' (258).

Therein lies the exciting challenge and, for some, the problem of biblical fictions. Novels fictionalising biblical characters can destabilise the relationship between the Bible and the arts. Their existence blurs the border between biblical narrative and fictionalised Bible stories, and that will worry some Christian readers while exciting others because it opens up the way for the narratives to host new interpretations. Because readers can read back into biblical narratives what they have read in fictionalised accounts (and vice versa), the border between them has become porous and permeable. This can be creative, but there are tensions. What distinction remains between fact and fiction? Although

I was taught in primary school that fiction is make-believe, I was also taught, misleadingly, that it is 'not true'. That assumption prevails for many people, although it ignores the nature of truth, in a discourse when we might want to distinguish between historicity and theological truth. Is it ever possible to discover precisely what actually happened in the events recounted in the books of the Bible? When we read biblical fiction, at what point can we be sure fiction has been introduced into the narrative? Richard Beard's recent novel, *Lazarus is Dead* (2011), explores these problems. It intentionally bends genres in that, throughout the novel provocatively subtitled *A Biography*, scholarly New Testament commentary, literary reworkings of the story and academic reflections by respected actual theologians mingle with the original biblical references to tell a new story of Lazarus. These citations, carefully italicised with the year of publication added and often discussed in essay-like digressions, help Beard in his apparent aim to resurrect Lazarus as a significant messianic contender, who, he tells readers, is commemorated in a minor festival eight days before Easter in churches of the Byzantine tradition. Readers of the novel cannot avoid questioning the relationship between novel and biography, as well as the nature of truth in Beard's new story of Lazarus. Beard himself straddles the divide between the Bible and fiction. On the one hand, through his novel he raises the possibility that the Bible could be fiction (150), and throughout the book insights from fiction fill out the biblical story (221); but, on the other hand, he suggests that because theology has reached 'A point of stagnation. . . . A new approach is needed' (246), one that allows for imaginative representations and reconfigurations of the narrative to fund the reader's reception of the story.

* * *

Beard's novel is so genre-bending that it merits further consideration in the form of a case study. At an early stage in the novel, Beard speculates about the death of Lazarus. If he were raised, he must have died, he argues, and if he died, he must have died of something! He writes,

> We've established that Lazarus's illness is so familiar that the Bible doesn't need to describe it. Also that Lazarus falls sick at the exact moment the water at the wedding in Cana becomes wine. None of the diseases common in the region at the time, however, fit the one-year interval between infection and death.

The incubation periods don't add up, and in this area the story of Lazarus needs some attention to make it credible. Even outside the story, beyond time, with the benefit of hindsight and foresight, it can be difficult to fit together.

It is therefore worth searching out more detailed evidence of the disease that plays its part and will eventually kill him.

'Nearly all his life he suffered from a weak heart, then he was cured, as everyone in Bethany could testify, and now he is dead.' José Saramago claims that Lazarus had chronic heart trouble, and died peacefully in his sleep.

Equally absurdly, the Czech writer Karel Capel (*Lazarus*, 1949) thinks Lazarus died of a chill – 'it was the cold wind that got me, that time when – when I was so ill . . .'

Not so. The story demands that Lazarus suffer. The more hideous his death the more impressive his revival. When the time comes, Jesus needs everyone to believe that Lazarus has truly come back to life. But they first need to believe, without reservation, that he died.

The most effective way to publicise his death in advance was to make his physical decline visible. His sickness should be horrific, definitive, undeniable. It should be both recognisable and worse than anything anyone has ever seen.

Yes, this is how it was done. Lazarus did not die from one of the seven prevalent illnesses of ancient Israel. Not enough. He has to contract them all (pp. 55-6).

Beard's citation of earlier novelists sets his own novel within a literary tradition and adds authority to the idea he is promoting that Lazarus died an awful death, for he argues against the earlier texts. Beard ploughs this furrow a little deeper when he refers to a 'thriving folk memory of a sick and diseased Lazarus' (58). It is as if Lazarus's illness migrates from the time before he dies to after his resuscitation, so that he is never fully recovered, but only half-alive. Beard notes Kazantzakis's use of this notion when, in *The Last Temptation*, he describes Lazarus's 'two yellow arms, cracked and full of dirt [and] finally the skeleton-like body' (58).

Later Beard refers to Lazarus's presence in a made-up Bible story – the only parable Jesus told with a named character:

During his ministry Jesus makes one public pronouncement about Lazarus. The message is encoded, and it confounds a Roman *speculatore* as completely as scholars down the centuries.

This is Roger Hahn from *The Voice*, an internet source of Bible commentary: 'Lazarus is the name applied to the poor beggar in the parable of The Rich Man and Lazarus in Luke 16: 19-31. However there appears to be no connection between the literary figure in the parable of Mary and Martha.'

There are many observers, even within the Church, who prefer to deny the each of Lazarus, and his unique ability to discomfort Jesus. They don't want Lazarus to be fully alive before he dies, because this can distract from what others see as the more important resurrection. Look. It's obvious.

'At his gate was laid a beggar named Lazarus, covered with sores and longing to eat what fell from the rich man's table. Even the dogs came and licked the sores' (Luke 16:20-21)

Jesus rarely names the characters in his parables. Here he makes an exception, and chooses the name of his only identified friend. This Lazarus, too, the one in the parable, is sick and dying. Coincidence? Remember that a parable is fiction, and Jesus can determine every element in the story.

Lazarus' is not a name picked at random, the first that enters his head. It is chosen for a reason. Think it through, analyse the coincidence (pp. 94-5).

When we analyse the coincidence and think why the sick and sore-covered man in the parable is also called Lazarus, we might consider what this says about the relationship between fiction and truth. The phrases 'the truth of fiction' and 'the fiction of truth' take on interesting connotations. Throughout the novel, Beard has blended his own narrative with references to literary scholars, theologians and biblical scholars, including footnotes as if the novel is non-fiction. Then towards the end, the novelist steps out of his narratival voice and addresses his readers directly, saying, 'A point of stagnation has been reached in scholarly and theological studies. A new approach is needed, and imaginative representations are an undervalued source of data. Evidence can be extrapolated through careful research, making a significant contribution to the sum of our knowledge' (246). This is what I am also arguing for in this book – a new approach to the making of our theologies, fresh insights into God from the perspective of literature, and the employment of imagination in our perception of the divine.

* * *

Blurring the boundary between the Bible and fiction, allowing biblical stories to veer away from the canon and slide into the marginalia of the non-canonical by recasting scripture as literature, as all these novels do, carries implications for the status of scripture, literature and narrative. First, what if the biblical text is as fictional as novels are? Because no narrative is entirely innocent, it is already acknowledged that the Bible's stories are not straight. There are elements of fiction in them. The histories of the Old Testament are formally known as 'the Former Prophets' because historians such as the Chronicler and the Deuteronomist were, above all else, theologians and prophets whose overt intention in recording their histories was to make theological claims and prophetic judgements: long-lived kings who were 'bad' in that they were unfaithful, impious or broke God's law in some way, are passed over in a sentence, while short-lived and politically insignificant kings who were faithful and obedient are given fuller attention. Inconsistent legends about the selection of David as king are difficult to reconcile – in one he is chosen from among his seven brothers when he is called back from tending his family's sheep, in another he is chosen because his music can soothe the furrowed brow of Saul, and in another he is chosen because he killed Goliath. The only way these can be reconciled is if, as is possible, the biblical historian has introduced three different narratives to stress that David is, at one and the same time, a shepherd who will be a pastor to his people, a harpist who will hymn God's praises in psalmody and a warrior who will protect his people from danger. The people of biblical times knew little of objective, disinterested history. The biblical authors and editors use many literary techniques, each of which introduces fictionalising elements, to explicate their theological, spiritual, ethical or religious purpose. The practice continued into the New Testament. The very nature of the Gospels – they are not biographies of Jesus, but proclamations of good news, propaganda in a non-pejorative sense – demonstrates that biblical narrative, in common with all narrative, is inflected. As David Jasper said when discussing Crace's *Quarantine*, 'all literature . . . plays with other texts and fictions which have influenced it, consciously or unconsciously'.[8] The Gospels are no exception: the four Evangelists crafted their stories with an ear to Old Testament echoes, sometimes directly citing texts from the prophets and specifying that what happened was 'so that the scripture can be fulfilled', but more often simply allowing readers to discern the allusion for themselves.

The pericope of Jesus's miraculous feeding of the multitude can serve as a helpful first example, partly because, unlike most accounts of Jesus

8. Jasper, (2004), p. 103.

as a miracle worker, versions of this narrative occur in all four Gospels. Both Matthew's and Mark's Gospels include an additional variant of the story, and, although detailed analysis is beyond the scope of this chapter, enough can be said to demonstrate how intertextuality plays with historicity and adds fictionality to the episode. Mark explains that Jesus looks with compassion on the people because they were like sheep without a shepherd (6:34), echoing an image criticising leaderless Israel used in Numbers, 1 Kings and Ezekiel. The collection of basketfuls of waste at the end of the miracle is reminiscent, but an exaggeration, of a story about Elisha told in 2 Kings 4, and the Fourth Gospel further heightens this allusion in its distinctive depiction of the boy as παιδάριον (paidarion), a term of uncertain meaning, possibly indicating a child servant, and used nowhere else in the New Testament. This, according to Barrett, probably originated in John's recollection of the same Elisha narrative, where the prophet was assisted by a servant.[9] The accounts, if contemporaneous with the action, also carry impossible forward-looking allusions, inasmuch as they have Eucharistic overtones when Jesus took the bread, looked to heaven, blessed and broke the loaves and gave them to his disciples who then gave them to the crowds. Such knowing intertextuality makes claims for the identity and nature of Jesus – that was its purpose – but it also troubles the historicity of the accounts.

If this suggests that reading biblical narratives as fiction helps us find within them theological or spiritual truths greater than mere historicity, the suggestion can be further reinforced by looking at the accounts of the Transfiguration. The story is so reminiscent of Moses's ascent of Sinai and so peppered with imprecise Old Testament allusions that many commentators find it difficult to avoid the conclusion that here is a narrative imaged (or imagined) in such a way that, above all else, it expresses what Mark and his readers believed about Jesus – that he was God's beloved son. In the process, fiction and 'historical "happening"', to use Morna Hooker's term, have been fused together in the narrative so firmly that they can no longer be separated.[10]

What implications, if any, do biblical fictions have on the way we read the Bible? When we read a Bible story, the element of the story with which readers engage most creatively is the fiction within and around the facts, rather than the facts within the fiction (although it is to be conceded that, for many Christians, historical fact is important). Just as our capacity to imagine is central to our ability to read a novel, the creative faculty we call imagination facilitates theological

9.   Barrett, (1978), pp. 274-5.
10. Hooker, (1991), p. 214.

understanding, enables us to find our place in the narrative and facilitates spiritual involvement. It is this that lifts the narrative out of the past, away from a distant land and into our lives here and now. This interplay between fiction and imagination when reading a Bible story should not disturb Christian believers; it need not even disturb biblical literalists; it certainly did not bother the biblical literalist John Milton, or deter him from his fictionalisation of the Fall in *Paradise Lost*. Reading the Bible as fiction need not reduce the status of the Bible as Christianity's sacred and authoritative text. Rather, if the Bible is read as fiction – or, to use this book's more provocative term from childhood, if it is read as 'make-believe' – the text is liberated from a specific period and place to everywhere and all time. It becomes a present reality that encourages belief. Why should people be surprised if the Gospel writers turned to fiction to do justice to their understanding of Jesus, just as Jesus himself turned to short stories, in the form of parables, to get his hearers to understand the content of his teaching and the nature of his being? Stories narrate truth. As Douglas Templeton argued in his book on reading the New Testament, 'To lose the Bible as history is not to *lose truth*, but to lose one *kind of it and find another*',[11] and this other theological, spiritual and religious truth reaches further and deeper into the reader than mere historical happenings. Reading the Bible as fiction energises scripture. Indeed, modern biblical fiction, by the accretion of further interpretative layers, opens up the Bible for readers to whom it may have previously been an alien text.

The biblical fiction genre has the further implication that literature can be read as scripture, that is, as an authoritative text capable of carrying religious truth. In the latter years of the twentieth century and the early years of the twenty-first, commentators often remarked on people's disaffection with organised religion while retaining a strong sense of spirituality. The spiritual curiosity that continues to characterise Western society often finds expression in popular interest in the arts because, in the absence of participation in corporate acts of worship, people look elsewhere for the aesthetics and artistic stimulation that 'feed the soul'. They visit art galleries, attend musical recitals, listen to poetry readings, read books, watch drama and film, and follow football clubs. Novels that retell stories from the Bible provide continuing access to narratives that have been formative in the past and that still establish norms for theistic belief, ethical behaviour and spiritual practice. For some, literature, with its imaginative, almost supernatural, power that demands leaps of faith from its readers to unleash its magic, has replaced

11. Templeton, (1999), p. 327.

the old religion. The divine can be found and heard in literature's beauty, truth and goodness. Perhaps also in its ugliness, lies and wickedness, for the divine may also be discernible in absence.

Fiction is as capable of holding authority as any other text, in that authority is never intrinsic to a text but negotiated by three interested parties – the writer, the reader and the text itself. This means that textual authority should never be coercive or absolute, but is either attributed to a text by its reader or agreed between the reader and author. Even a widely recognised and authoritative text such as the Bible cannot impose or force its authority; it can be ignored or disagreed with, and it only becomes authoritative when the reader agrees to read it as such. Readers of biblical fiction may choose to read novels in the same way, attributing to them either an authority from which they can learn how to behave or an authority from which they can discover theological or religious insights. Thus, novels with Jesus as a central character may inspire readers to follow his lifestyle or convey insights into the nature of Christian belief about him. Kazantzakis's *The Last Temptation of Christ*, for instance, offers important corrective insights into the doctrine of the incarnation and Saramago's Marxist version of Jesus's story encourages readers to judge Jesus by his life, rather than by the Church of his followers, and perhaps then to follow him. I welcome novels based on Bible stories because they liberate theology from the grip of the guardians of orthodoxy, patriarchal religion and the established church, and move theology back into the public realm where debate, dispute and quarrel, rather than privileged dominance, establish what is true.[12] Our openness to textual interpretation need not conflict with reverence for sacred texts.

Finally, if, as this chapter argues, the genre of biblical fiction implies that scripture can be read as literature and literature as scripture, it has a further effect: it heightens the role of narrative, for it emphasises that narrative carries theology and reminds believers that the stories of the Bible are, indeed, stories. Moreover, these stories are inconclusive stories, kept open by biblical fictions that prevent their closure.[13] In the last thirty or forty years, as I indicated in the opening chapter, a strand of theology dubbed 'narrative theology' has emerged, bolstered by the belief that all stories are essentially and unavoidably theological. This strand of theology places the burden of theological reflection on

---

12. Salman Rushdie, in an essay collected in his *Imaginary Homelands*, distinguished between religion whose tendency is to privilege one language above all others and novels where different languages, narratives and values quarrel.

13. Fisch makes a similar point when discussing how biblical narratives remain alive for future generations in the first chapter of his book (1998), p. 4.

narrative's shoulders. It is no accident, for instance, that much of the Torah – the books of the Old Testament that contain the Mosaic Law – is in the form of narrative, for our stories teach morality, establish norms and give theological instruction. Simply because narrative unfolds in an ordered manner, and because narrators tell stories for a reason, narrative promises to make sense of what it narrates and, when it reflects life as it is lived, it offers hope that life makes sense. People tell stories because they want to communicate what they have learnt and because they want to inculcate values by which they believe the hearer should live. Perhaps they want to make-believe. These are also the tasks or purposes of confessional theology. Narrative theology and the power of narrative meet in the genre of biblical fictions. In this meeting of story and theology there lies great potential because, especially in the genre of biblical fiction, narrative works as a valued tool in the theological task and reading fiction becomes a fruitful way of doing theology. Through these stories readers may find themselves approaching the ineffable, touching the hem of divinity's garment and learning more of God.

Chapter 9

RE-ENCHANTING A DISENCHANTED WORLD

We have looked at several genres of the contemporary novel – literary novels, science fiction, dystopia, fantasy, historical fiction, detective stories, novels by atheist writers and biblical fiction – and now we return to the question that took us on this quest: why does contemporary British fiction persist in pursuing theological themes, in exploring spirituality and in representing religious activities? Why the continued interest? And what does this persistence promise contemporary readers and their world?

The often frustrating paradox of religious faith is that, as a potential force for the betterment of humankind, it also bears the capacity to cause great damage. Religions can benefit people and do good, but they can also cause harm. Faith, usually intended to promote harmony, can be a source of division between people. What can improve one person's wellbeing can also introduce to that same person's life intolerance of difference and an arrogant sense of superiority. A religion that claims to be true all too readily claims absolute and exclusive truth. As a consequence, religion has probably been more destructive than any other force, and, both historically and currently, the story of religion in the world is peppered with atrocity. Some will observe this and choose to reject religion as a tool used by evil or misguided men and women to try to impose their doctrinaire ways on others. Many more, though, continue to profess a religious faith. About three-quarters of the world's current population confess religious beliefs. That proportion is projected to increase at least until the year 2050, and this is not only because children are being born to believing families, but because new people are being attracted. Those who make a life choice in favour of religion will often be aware of religion's paradox and may have concluded that what makes religion a force for harm is not bad theology or religion per se. For them, unlike atheists, the answer to bad theology is not no theology, but to develop good theology.

In disenchanted Britain, where church reaches fewer people than ever before, I find that literature has a role to play both in the critique of bad theology and in the development of good theology. As I write this final chapter, the Swedish Academy is meeting in unusual circumstances to deliberate over which two people should receive the Nobel Prize for Literature in 2019. Ever since 1901, this award has been awarded annually, but in 2018 a scandal prevented an award being made. I find it interesting that when Alfred Nobel founded the Nobel Prize as part of his atonement for being an arms manufacturer, he gave literature equal standing with the sciences and peace-making. He saw that literature has a critical role in the ecology of human behaviour and chose to use his Prize to promote its work. The modern juries who award the Prizes must share his view if they want to make good last year's gap. An anonymous journalist's comment on this was to observe that the world needs literature, and literature needs to be seen, cherished and honoured because it matters.[1] In my view, the world needs literature all the more in the twenty-first century than it did at the beginning of the twentieth because good religion is weakened and perverted forms threaten us.

Neil MacGregor, Director of the British Museum from 2002 to 2017, recently curated an exhibition that spawned a thirty-part series of radio programmes and a beautifully illustrated book, each entitled *Living with the Gods*. MacGregor used ancient and modern artefacts, the oldest from 40,000 years ago and the latest from 2013, to explore the connections between structures of belief and the structure of human society. The unifying theme of the exhibition of disparate items from so many different eras, cultures and religions was MacGregor's recognition of religious impulses common to humankind. These include the desire to ward off evil, the need to mark the initiation of a child into adulthood, the desire to visit sacred places of pilgrimage, and the phenomenon of gathered congregations collecting encouragement and strength from each other. Lucy Beckett, reviewing the book, discerned an elegiac tone in MacGregor's text. She asked, 'If religion binding society together is as ancient as anything we can discover about the human race, what do we miss if we find ourselves in a society that has left it behind?'[2] The loss of religion would be a real loss, she said, because we would lose its efforts to achieve human solidarity, unselfishness and kindness in individuals, and the quest for the virtues of justice and mercy. We would also, as a byproduct, gain the advantage

---

1. *The Guardian*, 9 March 2019, p. 2.
2. Beckett, Lucy, (2018), p. 32-3.

of losing perverted and distorted forms of religion, such as modern fundamentalisms that most, except their fervent adherents, believe should be defeated.

Because a natural affinity exists between fiction and religion, religion helps novelists explore the nature of their art, for both are reliant on narrative and imagination. By embedding religious texts in novels, by creating characters who place great store in the scriptures of their particular faith, and by discussing how the beliefs of contemporary characters relate to those of their ancestors, novelists problematise the concept of authoritative texts. Readers have to think about the nature of inspiration, the question of how, if at all, the text manages our beliefs and practices, and the nature of authorship and its relationship with authority. Through narrative – in history, liturgy and fiction – we attribute both meaning and order to our personal experience as well as to the overall experience of humankind. The stories make us believe that there could be purpose and meaning to human existence. Novelists can challenge wrongly told stories, they can recraft over-familiar stories whose power has dwindled and they can thereby call out bad forms of religion. They can be among the priests and prophets of our time. They can forge good theology and challenge religious behaviour calculated to cause harm. At their best, both religion and literature establish the reality of mystery and plumb the depths of human significance, thereby making us more human. For the sake of humanity and our future, therefore, we need novelists prepared to write of God and belief more than ever before.

We should note that each genre discussed in previous chapters sustains interest in religion, theology and spirituality for reasons specific to that genre. Science fiction uses religion to make a different future for its characters. Often, for science fiction writers, the real world is a liminal place that borders on other more wonderful places that, as in Wilson's *Alif the Unseen*, may be more than double the scale of the visible world. In such imagined worlds, science fiction often employs religious practices as community shapers. My chapter on science fiction, for instance, studied how the characters in Chris Beckett's Eden trilogy used religion to give existential meaning and shape to their community, and Michel Faber's *The Book of Strange New Things* warned what can happen when a society is dislocated from its faith.

Fantasy has always contributed to the religious imagination and writers have used fantasy to teach theology and promote ethical behaviour based on faith. But can fantasy make readers believe in God? Both dystopias and utopias undoubtedly share common ground with apocalyptic literature, and the suspension of disbelief required when reading fantasy suggests a turn towards God, but perhaps the most that can be achieved in such literature is that fantasy's imaginativeness creates a sense of wonder and marvel in the, perhaps God-given, strength of humanity.

Ian Mortimer's *The Outcasts of Time* epitomised, in its travel through several centuries, the way historical fiction often uses religion to contextualise narratives. Other novels studied in the chapter raised important issues about the impact of our religious history on the contemporary religious and political scene, and we also saw the danger facing novelists of assuming people of former ages were less theologically or spiritually advanced than we are.

Detective fiction relies on the trustworthiness of its narratives of crime, and judgement relies on the predicate of a moral universe. Ordinarily, in fiction published in English, this moral universe is informed by the Judeo-Christian religious tradition.

Atheistic writers seem unable to avoid religion as an inevitable preoccupation of the human race that cannot help but retain traces of religiosity. It is as if they feel challenged and compelled to write about what cannot be written about, and to speak of that for which no words are adequate. Their work becomes a quarrel over God and squabbles over whether religions harm or benefit humankind.

Many writers are attracted to the narratives of sacred texts including the Jewish and Christian Bibles, ancient mythologies and Eastern scriptures, not only because their themes are irresistible and the stories are so rich, but also because they raise fascinating questions about the truth and authority of sacred texts. Their retellings dislocate the narratives, thereby troubling and giving them new life.

Today's world is conscious of having once been a religious world, and the sacred has not entirely left even those who stay away from churches and other places of worship. Many retain a sense of standing on holy ground and find the world a 'thin place' with windows into what lies beyond. As organised religion draws back from many people's daily practices, other aspects of human existence – such as literature, film, sport, enjoyment of the outdoors and so on – step into the vacuum it leaves behind. Yet the crowds that flock to follow these pursuits in art galleries and bookshops go not just in search of a meaning the church no longer conveys, but because they are genuinely interested in the remnants of the disappearing religious world. They have heard rumours of angels and want to discover whether there is any truth in them. There remains a sense of God as an absence that is presence and a presence that is absent, an Otherness whom the poet R.S. Thomas said has always just left the room we enter, leaving behind no more than a lingering perfume of holiness.[3]

Writing of secular fine art, one theologian, Tim Gorringe, suggested that contemporary visitors to art galleries may still find that art speaks of the elusive but pressing mystery of the world, and provokes them to thought, wonder and even worship.[4] Similarly, novel-readers touch the edge of glory, glimpse mystery and are provoked to wonder, love and praise.

Novelists have stepped into the gaps vacated by organised religion. They partially fill those gaps. They also pick up the roles previously performed by the religious institutions. They, along with other artists and musicians working in a wide range of media, have become the priests and prophets of the modern age for many who are estranged from traditional religion. I encourage church book groups and individual believers to read novels – Christianly and religiously – because those who have hitched their wagons to some form of religion do well to pay heed to what these modern-day priests and prophets say.

* * *

To this point, one popular and voguish genre has evaded our attention. And yet this so-far absent genre is an attractive prospect for novelists who want to explore the phenomena of religious or spiritual experiences.[5] This is the genre of magical realism, sometimes known as magic realism or marvellous realism. On the basis of the analysis of the novels in previous chapters, as I have pursued the question of why novelists persist in portraying God and godly matters in their novels, I now posit a double-headed theory. First, magical realism is the natural milieu for convincingly communicating in fiction experiences by which characters come to know the miraculous, marvellous or numinous. Second, writers writing of God, religious belief and practices are unavoidably creating a form of magical or marvellous realism, which may, in some instances, be better called 'mysterious' realism.

First, however, I must sound a note of caution, for these are highly contested terms, made all the more contestable because they are applied not only to literature, but also to other art forms, and identified as being present in literature from several disparate literary cultures, most

---

3. 'The Absence' *Collected Poems 1945-1990*, p. 361.
4. Gorringe, (2011), pp. 192-3.
5. Dickinson, (2013), p. 97.

famously South America and post-colonial fiction. Because magical realism is closely related to science fiction, fantasy, fairy tales and allegory, defining the borders around the genre is a matter of further critical dispute. Complicating my argument even more is the fact that one of the best-known proponents of the art form in British literature is Salman Rushdie, and we have identified him as an atheist novelist in a previous chapter.

I am not the first to close a book about contemporary fiction and religion by turning to magical realism. Andrew Tate's chapter concluding *Contemporary British Fiction* expresses surprise that the contemporary novel has become a space in which sacred and secular concerns converge, but acknowledges that this is both the product of a 'sacred turn' and the outcome of an era when conventional theological and spiritual ideas are now explored outside conventional religious forums.[6] He shows how magical realism makes the occurrence of remarkable and wonderful events seem natural in novels that are keen to advocate that mystery lies behind the visible world, or that human existence is a commingling of the marvellous and the quotidian. I agree with Tate that magical realism is a handy tool for novelists touching on traditional transcendent theology, but further questions suggest themselves. In non-theological terms, it is plain that magical realism helps novelists insert a sense of wonder into their novels, but, can we go further and ask, does magical realism permit the presence of the supernatural and transcendent in novelistic accounts of the quotidian and mundane? When God enters novels does the portrait of divinity in fiction inevitably introduce elements of this literary genre?

The typical characteristics of magical realism suggest possible affirmative answers to these questions. First, magical realism depends on the accepted coexistence of two realms – natural and supernatural, reality and irreality – or, as Salman Rushdie said in *Midnight's Children*, the mundane and improbable commingle (9). Because both realms are given equally serious treatment by the author, the reader also accepts each at the same level. This characteristic distinguishes magical realism from its neighbouring genres of science fiction, fantasy and fairy tales, where the 'real' realm is underprivileged because the narratives are set in worlds other than the real one we can recognise around us now. Magical realism relies on the author's use of a matter-of-fact tone when non-realistic elements are presented, thus tending to denaturalise the real and naturalise the marvellous. While magical realism depends on the close proximity and the near-mergence of both realms, the inexplicability of

6. Tate, *op. cit.,* p. 126.

the supernatural remains throughout the text. The narrator, for instance, must never awake from a dream, for then the novelist has privileged the real over the fantastic. The oxymoronic nature of the term 'magical realism' hints at the further characteristic that it tends towards being subversive and transgressive in that, in juxtaposing the two realms, each brings the other into question. Moreover, magical realism often disturbs received ideas about time, space and identity, thus challenging the assumptions of the culture most dominant in the context into which the novel is published. Thus, it subverts any attempts to establish hegemony. Zamora and Faris suggest that magical realism enjoys an essential 'in-betweenness and all-at-onceness' that encourages resistance to any hegemonic or monological political or cultural structure.[7] These phrases – in-betweenness and all-at-onceness – express the commingling and the immanence of both the natural and supernatural worlds in magical realism. We should also note that magical realism admits the possibility of the plurality of worlds, or at least of worldviews, so texts often locate themselves on the liminal territory between or among such worlds. Commonly, the combination of these characteristics will unsettle readers and introduce into their minds a degree of doubt about the nature of the text before them.

Maggie Ann Bowers's concise guide to magical realism makes three further observations pertinent to my argument. The first alludes to Philip Swanson's suggestion that, in Isabel Allende's *The House of the Spirits* (1982), the spiritualism exercised by Clara represents once-happy times now destroyed by natural and political events, and that, to this extent, the world of the spirits portrays the ideal world towards which the real world should aspire.[8] Such critical engagement between the spiritual and natural realms, while not an essential feature of magical realism, is always possible in the genre. Mystery, transcendence and supernaturalism offer memories of lost innocence and the prelapsarian era; they also call us forward to work and hope for a better world and better times, because, as Wonderland's White Queen truthfully, though nonsensically, said, it is a curious form of memory that only works backwards.

Second, Bowers distinguishes between ontological and epistemological forms of magical realism. In the former, the source material for the beliefs and practices within the magical elements of the text originates in the cultural context of the novel. Epistemological magical realism takes inspiration from sources other than that context. To illustrate the distinction, Bowers refers to two magical realist writers in particular.

7.   Zamora and Faris, (1995), p. 6.
8.   Bowers, (2004), pp. 73-4.

In the case of the ontological form, she mentions Alejo Carpentier's *The Kingdom of this World* (1949) and his use therein of the Haitian belief that a man can change shape, a belief derived from a recognised Caribbean mythology, Carpentier writes of a shape-shifting character named Mackandal who can even take the form of an animal. We might also think of Salman Rushdie's use of *djinns* as coming from the cultural context of his novels. In the other group, Bowers cites a Flemish writer, Hugo Lampo, who drew his magical realist sources from Roman and Greek mythology. Although Bowers recognises an argument could be put that these mythologies are part of the culture of Lampo's novels because they had a profound and lasting effect on European cultures, the distance of time and geography between these mythologies and 1990s Belgium leads her to argue that Lampo drew his magical realism from sources other than Flemish folklore with its Germanic roots.[9] This prompts me to ask: is irreality akin or alien to reality? Where does the theological content of the novels in this study come from, from within our culture or from alien sources?

Finally, Bowers observes that, contrary to Toni Morrison's claim that she cannot be regarded as a magical realist writer because she does not have a culture to write out of, Morrison nevertheless writes magical realism 'inspired by the residual influence of the belief systems of . . . African American slaves'. These men and women had been forced to abandon their own languages and beliefs to adopt the English language and Christian beliefs, but some exchanges across the cultures took place. For example, some of Morrison's characters can fly back to Africa when they die, and this, Bowers says, is a common notion among eighteenth- and nineteenth-century African American slaves.[10] Is this dependence upon the residue of belief systems what goes on when theological content is part of contemporary novels? Are the religious, theological and spiritual features in modern novels, no more than a residual belief system, nothing more than the remnants of faith?

Even when the religious belief behind the element of the supernatural within a novel is so natural to the novelist as to be part of his or her background and culture, and believed by him or her, that supernatural element can be regarded as an instance of magical or marvellous realism in the text. Elements of the supernatural are one way to put the wonder back into a world many of us take for granted. They get us to see beyond what meets the eye. Perhaps they make us believe. In an essay about faith and magical realism, Christopher Warnes advised that when we ask three

---

9.   *ibid.*, pp. 91-2.
10. *ibid.*, p. 93.

questions to help us interpret magical realist texts – what is the source of the supernatural here, what is the nature of the relationship between the supernatural and the natural world at this point, and why has the author now resorted to this genre? – two characteristics of magical realism are displayed.[11] One is that the marvellous element unmasks the real and shows that the natural world is capable only of bearing provisional truths. The other is that, in challenging realism's claim to be able to explain and account for the world, the magical, supernatural element claims an equal right to do so.

Novelists with theological, religious or spiritual themes bring the supernatural and natural into coexistence within their texts in what we might call 'a state of contrived equivalence', thereby creating a form of magical, marvellous or mysterious realism. In other words, when elements of the divine or aspects of spirituality intrude into the text of a novel, and both the divine and the human realm have equal value, aspects of magical realism are present. The effect of this is that readers' eyes can be opened to whatever lies beyond the merely tangible. Magical realism re-enchants a disenchanted world and puts back the wonder.

* * *

In epilogue to this book, I turn to A.N. Wilson's recent novel, *Aftershocks* (2018), as a notable example of what religion in fiction can achieve in two respects. First, the novel represents Christianity as a polychrome faith and describes a range of possible responses Christians may make to certain shared experiences; and, second, it demonstrates a contemporary need for a shift in religious thought and shows its principal character making such a shift, thereby forging new and honest theology.

Set in a location simply known as the 'Island' in the antipodes, which has similarities with New Zealand, after a warning earthquake and during a major one, *Aftershocks* was inspired by the earthquake that hit Christchurch in 2011, but Wilson is at pains to state that the fictitious city of Aberdeen is not Christchurch, and that only one minor character – the town busker – is based on an actual person. Having spent only three weeks in New Zealand, he expresses himself unable to depict New Zealand in a novel. As has been the habit of this book, I will bring into the foreground some significant theological themes, but the novel is more than these themes: it has been called a paean to lesbian love, as its Sapphic narrator, who avoids using the 'L' word, is the central character's lover, Ingrid; it includes sections discussing ancient, classical

11. Warnes, (2005), pp. 5-6.

and contemporary literature because some of its characters are literary scholars, while others are actors and yet others are clergy who find sustenance in poetry; and it is an examination of a society disrupted, and almost destroyed, by political corruption, political ineptitude and natural disaster. *Aftershocks* is, at heart, Nellie and Ingrid's love story in the fictitious city of Aberdeen. Nellie is the Dean of Aberdeen Cathedral, who for the first part of the novel is presented as a personality torn between being an academic, referred to as Digby, and a cleric called Eleanor. Only when the earthquake strikes Aberdeen, killing 253 citizens, does Nellie discover the sense of integrity that enables her to combine these two aspects of her being. Being two people at once, one a clergyperson believing in God, the other a non-believing classicist, had somehow been a survival technique that kept her sane and balanced (162). However, after having been trapped in the cathedral tower when it collapsed and having suffered a fractured arm, ten days after the earthquake she prepares to lead worship outside the ruined cathedral in Argyle Square and she feels at one with herself: 'as a united being [she] felt strong to face life's paradoxes' (187). The story of this bifurcated individual can be read as an account of the trials and tribulations of being a free-thinking Christian. According to Ingrid, who envies the fact that Nellie had met Iris Murdoch, the setting of the novel is what Murdoch called the Time of the Angels, an age when belief in a personal God is no longer the norm, but when relics of the old religion, before it was 'all shook up', hang around, like angelic presences (59). Such a shaken-up world is the world into which all twenty-first-century novels are published.

The novel shows a variety of responses to the earthquake that was ferocious enough to shatter belief. After the first earthquake that later came to be seen as a warning of the big one yet to come, Bishop Dionne Lillicrap, irreverently nicknamed the Pontiff, preached in the cathedral. Readers have already noted the Dean's and the narrator's shared irritation at the Pontiff's managerial and theological simplicities. Because the names of all characters in novels are deliberately chosen, Wilson's choice of surname for the bishop probably flags up their irritation. In her sermon, after referring to the great damage another earthquake had inflicted on Aquila, she declares that the people of Aberdeen have been spared for a purpose. 'We could so easily have been wiped out. But that wasn't God's plan for us,' she says, leaving the narrator to ask, 'Was Dionne suggesting that the people of Aquila, who had been killed in some numbers . . . had deserved to be wiped out? And if they did not deserve it, why had God done this to them?' (99-100). This portrait of an interventionist, providential God who allows nothing to happen without purpose, and yet is prepared to act in ways that cause hurt, is far from uncommon among contemporary Christians. Yet to hold this view, does one require blinkers so that only the solipsistic particular is visible, only what affects 'me'? I have been saved, but what of those who did not survive?

Four alternative responses to the tragedy are represented in the novel through the arts. First, Doug, the Dean's ex-husband who had remained in England when she had moved to the Island to become Dean, sends an email on hearing of the earthquake enquiring after her wellbeing. Its almost uncaring brevity – 'You OK? Xx' – brings W.H. Auden's poem 'Musée des Beaux Arts' to Nellie's mind. Inspired by his visit to an art gallery and, in particular, by Breughel's depiction of the fall of Icarus, Auden notes that the old masters were never wrong about suffering. It took place while other people were 'eating or opening a window or just walking dully along'. As Icarus fell from the sky and splashed into the sea, the ploughman turned away, the sun shone on Icarus's pale legs and a delicate ship, whose crew must have seen something amazing, simply sailed calmly on. Doug is one of many who, not directly affected by the earthquake in Aberdeen, will choose to turn away and get on with their own lives as if nothing extraordinary had occurred.

The second literary response is an allusion to Henry Scott Holland, who, as a Canon of St Paul's Cathedral, responded to the death of King Edward VII in 1910 with a sermon, from which a paragraph has been rendered as a poem, often read at funerals. It begins 'Death is nothing at all.' In the immediate aftermath of the earthquake, Nellie attends over twenty funerals, four in one day, two of which she conducts. Her experience of overwhelming tragedy exposes the lie of Scott Holland's words, for she sees that in all the funerals in which this is read out, everything did not remain exactly as it had been, and death was a reality to be faced, not a nothing to be denied. She finds the poem callous in that it ignored the heartbreak of not being able to see the one you love. 'Hoping that you would meet in Heaven,' she thinks, 'was not, and could not, be the same thing as believing they had slipped out into the next room' (203). Scott Holland's words, ripped out of the context of the original sermon, now deny the pain of suffering, rather than express Christian hope for eternal life.

Earlier in the novel, Barnaby and Nellie plan a seminar on 'King Lear and the Gods'. The narrator's single wry comment on this is to quote from the play: 'As flies to wanton boys are we to the gods. They kill us for their sport' (120). Of all possible quotations, the choice of this contributes to the novel's critique of pietistic responses to tragedy. Are the gods, or God, playing cruelly with their creatures when the earth liquefies and shakes, causing such havoc and such pain? This is always a possible, if capriciously unorthodox, religious response.

Greek tragedy features in *Aftershocks* twice – once when Ingrid directs a performance of Euripides's *Trojan Women*, and, again, when Nellie prepares an academic paper on the 1971 film version of the same play. The significance of this play for the novel is that the play adds to the book's analysis of how humans respond to suffering, in that Euripides is 'unconstrained by monotheism. He did not have to believe in a loving God, or a creator God. He put the gods on stage and demonstrated the extent to which their frivolous malice was the cause of human misfortune' (153). Belief that God loves God's creatures lies at the heart of the problem of the Christian response to pain, what Muriel Speak simply called 'the only problem'.

Penny Whistle, the busker with the rich baritone voice who sings all day long without seeming to repeat himself, switches his repertoire from eighteenth-century English folk songs and ballads in response to the earthquake. As night falls on what the narrator calls 'this dreadful day', with clouds of dust still rising to fill survivors' lungs and the ground still shaking, Penny Whistle can be heard singing from John Newton's hymn, 'Amazing Grace':

> Through many dangers, toils and snares
> we have already come.
> 'Twas grace that brought us safe thus far
> and grace shall lead us home.

I suspect the narrator finds his familiar voice, as well as the words of Newton's hymn, comforting.

Set against these varied responses is the Dean's more challenging response. Trapped in the cathedral tower, feeling that 'coldfingered Death was very close' (158), she had had the coolness of mind to press 'Save' on the computer she was working on as the world crumbled around her, but she found that, unlike her father who would pray for her if he knew the predicament she was in, she had no recourse to prayer in this moment of extremis. She had no inclination to pray. She agonises over what sort of priest she can be if she does not pray, even at times like this. We see what sort of priest she is when she preaches ten days after the tragedy. For me, this sermon is the climax of the novel, marking a reimagining of God that I would like to see all theology in literature achieve.

The Dean had insisted on preaching as she was rostered for that day, and now stands before a shocked population. She begins with the attention-grabbing observation that 'Christianity came into being because a city was reduced to rubble' (187). The city she refers to is Jerusalem reduced to ruins by the Roman armies of Emperor Titus in 70 CE. In their current circumstances, her hearers will have greater ability to empathise with the inconsolability of those Jerusalem families who had endured such a devastating loss. The next move in the sermon is to biblical criticism as the Dean reminds the congregation that all four New Testament Gospels were written after the fall of Jerusalem, for each mentions its destruction. For them, the destruction of the Temple indicated the formation of a new religion in Jesus: 'A complete break with the past had occurred. Perhaps that's why, when Jesus died, there was an earthquake' (188). Only Matthew writes of this earthquake, and the Dean's explanation of this singular reference is that Matthew was announcing the beginning of the messianic age heralded by the opening of graves and a general resurrection. In other words, there is a theological rather than an historical reason for an account of an earthquake as Jesus died. The Dean asks what we are to make of this Stanley-Spencer-like image of people climbing out of their graves. She honestly does not know, and will not venture any rationalist suggestion, but she says she will offer 'a few thoughts' (189). She alludes to Jesus's cry of dereliction from the cross and likens it to the cry of the Trojan women in Euripides's tragedy, for it echoes the cry of all religious humanity whenever calamity strikes. She verbalises what she hears in the cries around her in Aberdeen: 'Why did my child, my lover, my father, have to die in this pointless way? Where is God when you need Him?' Wounded humanity has always called out in similar ways for justice and consolations. People have hoped that religious explanations will somehow make the pain easier to bear. Those who do not believe in God, she says, would not expect nature to be fair or kind or loving. At this point in her sermon, she declares that Aberdeen was not destroyed by God or the gods, but by 'blind Nature'. She hears in Jesus's cry of dereliction, and sees in the tearing in two of the Temple curtain, that the earthquake in Matthew's Gospel demolished the religious norms of the day.

The earthquake that hit Aberdeen similarly demands reimagined theology. 'It leaves us without the old God,' she says, 'The God that William Blake called Nobodaddy' (190). We must forsake this illusory God, she asserts, before encouraging her hearers to 'try to enter into what the first Christians discovered', which is that 'the glory of God can only shine out of a human face'. She wants her hearers to follow her in saying goodbye to the Temple, the legendary Jehovah and the immortal gods of Olympus and 'embrace instead the divinity within each human being' (190). The Dean does not worry about the historicity of the Gospels. Rather, she rejoices that she finds in them a 'rich set of stories, liberating [her] to become more human' (191). Discussion earlier in the novel, when Nellie had talked about the anarchic nature of the Gospels that she remembers Trevor Huddlestone had described as the most revolutionary text he could conceive (75), and when she had suggested that the experience of knowing God enjoys precedence as an authority for religious belief over that of the Bible, has prepared the reader for the Dean's constructive use of the Bible in this sermon. She concludes with an expression of hope that the city will pick itself up, and, through its people's capacity to believe in one another, build itself into 'an abode of love'.

In short, this sermon argues for a paradigm shift, and is therefore doing what sermons are meant to do. When they work, sermons change minds, hearts and lives. Part of preaching's transformative role lies in that sermons will prompt a reimagining of God, of others and of ourselves. Ingrid Ashe, at the beginning of the novel, had indicated that, far from being a story to make us believe in God, by the end of her story we will not be able to trust the ground we tread on. 'Religion itself,' she says, 'can never be quite the same' (16). Now, in the aftermath of the quake, we see this necessity for change. Ingrid's story is truly what she said it would be, the story of 'how an earthquake helped [her] find True Love' (6) or, in religious terms, 'a journey into Truth' (15), for, in the aftermath of tragedy as its aftershocks are still being felt, Nellie advises the people that they must think again about what they believe about God. God, she says, is not to be found in the forces of nature or in some male Creator figure, but Jesus shows that God shines out of a human face, and this, perhaps fresh, way of thinking has the potential to liberate us to be more human. That a critic of Nellie's had once alleged that she reduced Christianity to nothing higher than do-gooding does not deter Nellie in her reimagining of God. She cannot think of anything deeper than doing good, revering the Good and contemplating the Good. I am reminded of Iris Murdoch's equivalence of God with goodness, rendering the divinity as 'Go(o)d'. Our capacity to do good, Nellie says, distinguishes us from all that is evil, and she expresses astonishment that in the world's worst places – gulags and concentration camps – examples of outstanding forbearance and gentleness are often found (77). She expresses Christianity's central tenet of faith in terms of God discarding omnipotence to go about Palestine for a few short years doing good. 'Faith in the incarnation could not be detached, either from contemplation or from deeds of good' (77).

After the Dean's father dies, she returns to England, ostensibly for the funeral, but we suspect she will never return. There she dines with her father's old friend whom she knew as Uncle Lesley. She shares with him that she no longer believes in God. He reassures her that in herself 'all [she] has to do is be true' (258), and they laugh about the old motto of Cuddesdon, their theological college, as he and her father had previously often done. Translated into English, the motto urged believers 'To keep by the Holy Ghost which dwelleth in us that good thing which was committed unto thee.' What amused them was that they often rendered it as 'Guard the deposit.' This, however, is the appeal Wilson's novel makes: keep faithful, whatever happens and whatever one believes.

Concluding this book with *Aftershocks* is appropriate, for the central character in Wilson's novel makes a tectonic shift in her theology. She worries that she no longer believes in God. What has happened is that her deeply troubling experiences in New Zealand have shaken her understanding of God. Her faith has changed. What she now believes will sustain her amid the complexities of contemporary life. Implicitly, Wilson challenges readers to adopt mature and intelligent theology for twenty-first-century living. This study of God in recent fiction makes a similar challenge.

I believe the peculiar circumstances of twenty-first-century Britain – increasing secularity, changes in our multi-cultural context, lack of confidence in organised forms of belief, the offer of alternative lifestyles and challenging ethical issues – require fresh ways of talking about God. A shaken world requires shaken-up and shaken-down theology. Towards the end of last century, George Pattison argued for the need for dialogism to save theology from a threatened end. The need, post 9/11, is even more urgent. Because theology is beyond words in that they are inadequate in any talk about God, interaction with other disciplines – visual arts, dance, poetry, film being only a few of many – is essential for theology's continuing life. Such dialogism enriches our talk of God (theology), our practices to do with God (religion) and our thinking about God (spirituality). It is a faithful way of doing theology. Having spent many years using literature to do theology, I now find that God is like the hound of heaven, chasing me in long pursuit, down the arches of the years, night and day, through the labyrinths of my mind and my life experiences to wherever I may try to hide. I may choose to flee God, but never successfully, for I find God dancing across almost every page I read, making me think about why I believe what I believe and why I read as I do.

I have argued in this book that, despite being comprised of words, and despite telling lies in order to tell truth, fiction contributes to the enrichment of the Christian's engagement with the divine. This is because fiction tells stories, imagines characters and creates images, and, in so doing, it weaves a stronger theology to bring us closer to God. According to Sara Collins's character Frannie Langton, 'Novels make it possible to believe'.[12] The God I find dancing through novels re-enchants a disenchanted world, and this calls us to make a mind-shift in our thinking about God. I find myself believing in God who reveals Godself in all human experience including our culture, our literature and our fiction. This God speaks through our contemporary prophets and priests, including our contemporary novelists. Churches may continue to trot out old clichés, but soon they will be found wanting. We must allow ourselves to be honest as we adjust the way we think in the light of new knowledge, new reading and fresh experiences.

---

12. Collins, (2019), p. 369.

BIBLIOGRAPHY

A: Primary Sources

Arditti, Michael, (2018), *Of Men and Angels*, London: Arcadia
Beard, Richard, (2011), *Lazarus is Dead: A Biography*, London: Harvill Secker
Beckett, Chris, (2011), *The Holy Machine*, London: Corvus Books
——————, (2012), *Dark Eden*, London: Corvus Books
——————, (2015), *Mother of Eden*, London: Corvus Books
——————, (2016), *Daughter of Eden*, London: Corvus Books
Bray, Carys, (2014), *A Song for Issy Bradley*, London: Hutchinson
Brooks, Geraldine, (2008), *The People of the Book*, London: Harper
Catling, Brian, (2007), *The Vorrh*, Croydon: Honest Publishing
Faber, Michel (2014), *The Book of Strange New Things*, Edinburgh: Canongate
Griffiths, Neil, (2017), *As a God Might Be*, Buxton: Dodo Publishing Co
Harvey, Samantha, (2018), *The Western Wind*, London: Jonathan Cape
Hurley, Andrew Michael, (2014), *The Loney*, London: John Murray
——————, (2017), *Devil's Day*, London: John Murray
Laird, Nick, (2017), *Modern Gods*, London: HarperCollins
Martel, Yann, (2002), *Life of Pi*, Edinburgh: Canongate
McCarthy, Cormac, (2006), *The Road*, London: Picador
McCleen, Grace (2012), *The Land of Decoration*, London: Chatto and Windus
McEwan, Ian, (2005), *Saturday*, London: Vintage
——————, (2014), *The Children Act*, London: Vintage
Mortimer, Ian, (2017), *The Outcasts of Time*, London: Simon and Schuster
Parks, Tim, (2016), *Thomas and Mary: A Love Story*, London: Vintage
Perry, Sarah, (2016), *The Essex Serpent*, London: Serpent's Tail
Preston, Alex, (2012), *The Revelations*, London: Faber and Faber
Runcie, James, (2012), *Sidney Chambers and the Shadow of Death*, London:
    Bloomsbury
Rushdie, Salman, (2009), *The Enchantress of Florence*, London: Vintage
Underdown, Beth, (2017), *The Witchfinder's Sister*, London: Viking
Wilson, A.N., (2018), *Aftershocks*, London: Atlantic Books
Wilson, G. Willow, (2012), *Alif the Unseen*, London: Corvus Books
Wood, James, (2004), *The Book against God*, London: Vintage

B: Other Fiction and Poetry

Aidenhoff, Elsie V., (2006), *The Garden*, London: Doubleday
Allende, Isabel, [1982] (2011), *The House of Spirits*, London: Vintage
Atwood, Margaret, (1987), *The Handmaid's Tale*, London: Virago
——————, (2003), *Oryx and Crake*, London: Bloomsbury
——————, (2009), *The Year of the Flood*, London: Virago
——————, (2013), *MaddAddam*, London: Bloomsbury
Barker, Pat, (1996), *The Regeneration Trilogy*, London: Viking
Barnes, Julian, (1989), *A History of the World in 10½ Chapters*, London: Picador
Barry, Sebastian, (2005), *A Long, Long Way*, London: Faber and Faber
Borges, Jorge L., [1944] (1991), *Ficciones*, London: French and European
    Publications Inc
Brooks, Geraldine, (2001), *Year of Wonders: A Novel of the Plague*, London: Fourth
    Estate
Byatt, A.S., (1978), *The Virgin in the Garden*, London: Vintage
——————, (1985), *Still Life*, London: Vintage
——————, (1990), *Possession: A Romance*, London: Vintage
——————, (1996), *Babel Tower*, London: Chatto and Windus
——————, (2002), *A Whistling Woman*, London: Vintage
Carpentier, Alejo, (1949), *The Kingdom of this World*, New York: Alfred A. Knopf
Collins, Sara, (2019), *The Confessions of Frannie Langton*, London: HarperCollins
Crace, Jim, (1997), *Quarantine*, Harmondsworth: Penguin
Defoe, Daniel, [1719] (1988), *The Life and Adventures of Robinson Crusoe*, London:
    Marshall Cavendish
Diamant, Anita, [1997] (2001), *The Red Tent*, London: Macmillan
Dickinson, Michael, (1994), *The Lost Testament of Judas Iscariot*, Dingle: Brandon
Diski, Jenny, (2000), *Only Human*, London: Virago
——————, (2004), *After These Things*, London: Virago
Douglas, Lloyd C., (1942), *The Robe*, London: Peter Davies
——————, (1949), *The Big Fisherman*, London: Peter Davies
Elliott, Elissa, (2009), *Eve*, New York: Bantam
Faber, Michel, (2000), *Under the Skin*, Edinburgh: Canongate
——————, (2009), *The Fire Gospel*, Edinburgh: Canongate
Fielding, Henry, [1743] (1932), *The History of the Adventures of Joseph Andrews and
    His Friend Mr Abraham Adams*, London: G. Bell & Sons
Fowles, John, [1969] (2004), *The French Lieutenant's Woman*, London: Vintage
Graves, Robert, [1946] (1981), *King Jesus*, New York: Farrar, Straus and Giroux
Grossman, David, (2006), *Lion's Honey: The Myth of Samson*, Edinburgh:
    Canongate
Hanrahan, Gareth, (2019), *The Gutter Prayer*, London: Orbit
Jacobson, Dan, (1970), *The Rape of Tamar*, London: Andre Deutsch
Joyce, James, [1914] (1956), *The Dubliners*, Harmondsworth: Penguin
——————, [1922] (1969), *Ulysses*, Harmondsworth: Penguin
Kazantzakis, Nikos, (1975), *The Last Temptation*, London: Faber and Faber
Kennelly, Brendan, (1991), *The Little Book of Judas*, Tarset: Bloodaxe Books
Kohn, Rebecca, (2004), *The Gilded Chamber*, Harmondsworth: Penguin

Lamming, R.M., (2005), *As in Eden*, London: Faber and Faber
Levy, Andrea, (2004), *Small Island*, London: Review
Mailer, Norman, (1997), *The Gospel According to the Son*, London: Little, Brown
Maine, David, (2004), *The Flood*, Edinburgh: Canongate
————————, (2005), *Fallen*, Edinburgh: Canongate
————————, (2006), *The Book of Samson*, Edinburgh: Canongate
Massie, Allan, (1995), *King David*, London: Sceptre
Mawer, Simon, (2000), *The Gospel of Judas*, London: Little, Brown
McCaughrean, Geraldine, (2004), *Not the End of the World*, Oxford: Oxford
     University Press
McEwan, Ian, (2002), *Atonement*, London: Vintage
————————, (2008), *On Chesil Beach*, London: Vintage
McGregor, Jon, (2002), *If Nobody Speaks of Remarkable Things*, London:
     Bloomsbury
Michaels, Anne, (1997), *Fugitive Pieces*, London: Bloomsbury
Mitchell, David, (2014), *The Bone Clocks*, London: Sceptre
Moore, George, (1933), *The Brook Kerith: A Syrian Story*, London: William
     Heinemann Ltd
Murdoch, Iris, (1966), *The Time of the Angels*, London: Chatto and Windus
Pullman, Philip, (2010), *The Good Man Jesus and the Scoundrel Christ*, Edinburgh:
     Canongate
Rice, Anne, (2005), *Christ the Lord: Out of Egypt*, London: Chatto and Windus
————————, (2008), *Christ the Lord: The Road to Cana*, London: Chatto and
     Windus
Roberts, Michèle, (1984), *The Wild Girl*, London: Methuen
————————, (1999), *The Book of Mrs Noah*, London: Vintage
Rogers, Jane, (1991), *Mr Wroe's Virgins*, London: Faber and Faber
Rushdie, Salman, (1981), *Midnight's Children*, London: Vintage
Saramago, José, (1993), *The Gospel According to Jesus Christ*, London: The Harvill
     Press
Scott, Walter, [1814] (1981), *Waverley*, Oxford: Clarendon Press
Stead, C.K., (2006), *My Name was Judas*, London: Harvill Secker
Thomas, R.S., (2000), *Collected Poems 1945-1990*, London: Phoenix
Tremain, Rose, (1989), *Restoration*, London: Hamish Hamilton
Updike, John, (1975), *A Month of Sundays*, London: Andre Deutsch Ltd
Waters, Sarah, (2002), *Tipping the Velvet*, London: Virago
————————, (2003), *Fingersmith*, London: Virago
Winterson, Jeanette, (1985), *Boating for Beginners*, London: Vintage
Woolf, Virginia, [1925] (1964), *Mrs Dalloway*, Harmondsworth: Penguin

C: Secondary Criticism and Theology

Alter, Robert, (1981), *The Art of Biblical Narrative*, New York: HarperCollins
Armstrong, Philip, (2008), *What Animals Mean in the Fiction of Modernity*,
     Abingdon: Routledge
Barrett, C. Kingsley, (1978), *The Gospel According to St John: An Introduction with
     Commentary and Notes on the Greek Text, Second Edition*, London: SPCK

Beckett, Lucy, (2018), 'Homo Religiosus' in *The Times Literary Supplement*, 30
    November 2018, pp. 32-3
Booth, Wayne C., (1988), *The Company We Keep: An Ethics of Fiction*, Berkeley:
    University of California Press
Bowers, Maggie A., (2004), *Magic(al) Realism*, Abingdon: Routledge
Bradley, Arthur and Andrew Tate, (2010), *The New Atheist Novel: Fiction,
    Philosophy and Polemic after 9/11*, London: Continuum
Butterfield, Herbert, (1924), *The Historical Novel: An Essay*, Cambridge:
    Cambridge University Press
Cole, Stewart, (2004), 'Believing in Tigers: Anthropomorphism and Incredulity
    in Yann Martel's *Life of Pi*' in *Studies in Canadian Literature* Vol. 29 No. 2, pp.
    22-36
Cummins, Anthony, (2014), Review of *The Book of Strange New Things* by Michel
    Faber in *The Telegraph*, 6 November 2014
————————, (2018), Review of *The Western Wind* by Samantha Harvey, in *The
    Guardian*, 25 February 2018
Cunningham, David S., (2002), *Reading is Believing: The Christian Faith through
    Literature and Film*, Grand Rapids, Michigan: Brazos Press
Cunningham, Valentine, (2000), 'The Best Stories in the Best Order? Canons,
    Apocryphas and (Post)modern Reading' in *Literature and Theology*, 14/1, 69-
    80
Cupitt, Don, (1991), *What is a Story?* London: SCM
Cusack, Carole M., (2008), 'Scarlet and Black: Non-Mainstream Religion as
    "Other" in Detective Fiction' in *Sydney Studies in Religion*, pp. 1-16
Davie, Grace, (2015), *Religion in Britain: A Persistent Paradox*, Chichester: Wiley
    Blackwell
De Groot, Jerome, (2010), *The Historical Novel*, Abingdon: Routledge
Dickinson, David, (2013), *The Novel as Church: Preaching to Readers in
    Contemporary Fiction*, Baylor: Baylor University Press
————————, (2016), *Yet Alive? Methodists in British Fiction since 1890*,
    Newcastle upon Tyne: Cambridge Scholars Press
Feay, Suzi, (2017), Review of *The Witch Finder's Sister* by Beth Underdown in *The
    Guardian*, 17 March 2017
Feigel, Lara, (2017) Review of *As a God Might Be* by Neil Griffiths in *The
    Guardian*, 25 November 2017
Fiddes, Paul S., ed., (2000), *The Novel, Spirituality and Modern Culture: Eight
    Novelists Write about Their Craft and Their Context*, University of Wales Press:
    Cardiff
Fisch, Harold, (1998), *New Stories for Old: Biblical Patterns in the Novel*, London:
    Macmillan
Fischer, Steven R., (2003), *A History of Reading*, London: Reaktion Books
Gearon, Liam, ed., (1999), *English Literature, Theology and the Curriculum:
    Theology in Dialogue*, London: Cassell
Genders, Paul, (2016), 'As Himself' in *The Times Literary Supplement*, 26 February
    2016
Gorringe, Timothy, (2011), *Earthly Visions: Theology and the Challenges of Art*, Yale:
    Yale University Press

Green, Garrett, (1998), *Imagining God: Theology and the Religious Imagination,*
    Grand Rapids, Michigan: Wm. B. Eerdmans Publishing Co
Groes, Sebastian, ed., (2013), *Ian McEwan: Contemporary Critical Perspectives,*
    London: Bloomsbury
Harrison, M. John, (2018), Review of *The Western Wind* by Samantha Harvey in
    The Guardian, 1 March 2018
————————, (2018), Review of *Devil's Day* by Andrew Michael Hurley in *The
    Guardian,* 26 October 2017
Harrison, Melissa, (2018), Review of *The Western Wind* by Samantha Harvey in
    The Financial Times, 9 March 2018
Haynes, Stephen R., (1995), 'Footsteps of Ann Hutchinson and Frederick
    Buechner: A Religious Reading of John Irving's *A Prayer for Owen Meany*' in
    Religion and Literature, 27.3, pp. 73-98
Head, Dominic, (2007), *Ian McEwan: Contemporary British Novelists,* Manchester:
    Manchester University Press
Higdon, David L., (1984), *Shadows of the Past in Contemporary British Fiction,*
    London: Macmillan
Holton, Robert, (1994), *Jarring Witnesses: Modern Fiction and the Representation of
    History,* Hemel Hempstead, UK: Harvester Wheatsheaf
Hooker, Morna D., (1991), *The Gospel According to St Mark,* London: A & C
    Black
Hrotic, Steven, (2014), *Religion in Science Fiction: The Evolution of an Idea and the
    Extinction of a Genre,* London: Bloomsbury
Jasper, David, (2004), *The Sacred Desert: Religion, Literature, Art and Culture,*
    Oxford: Blackwell
Jeffrey, David L., ed., (1992), *A Dictionary of Biblical Tradition in English
    Literature,* Grand Rapids: Eerdmans
————————, (1996), *People of the Book: Christian Identity and Literary Culture,*
    Grand Rapids: Eerdmans
Kaufman, Gordon D., (1981), *The Theological Imagination: Constructing the
    Concept of God,* Philadelphia: Westminster Press
Keates, Jonathan, (2017), 'Spiritual Home: Integrity and Multitudes in an
    Unapologetically Theological Novel' in *The Times Literary Supplement,* 15
    December 2017, p. 22
Keefer, Kyle, (2008), *The New Testament as Literature: A Very Short Introduction,*
    Oxford: Oxford University Press
Kelly, Stuart, (2017), Review of *The Erstwhile* in *The Guardian,* 25 March 2017,
    p. 9
Kibble, David G., (2019), 'New Directions in Relating Christianity to Other
    Faiths' in *Theology* Vol. 122/1, pp. 30-7
Kim, Julie H., (2005), *Race and Religion in the Post-colonial British Detective Story:
    Ten essays,* London: Macfarlane & Co
Kraemer, David, (1996), *Reading the Rabbis: The Talmud as Literature,* Oxford:
    Oxford University Press
Küng, Hans, (1976), *On Being a Christian,* London: Collins
————————, (1993), *Credo: The Apostles' Creed Explained for Today,* London:
    SCM Press

Lapointe, Michael, (2018), 'Sodom and Torah' in *The Times Literary Supplement*, 4 May 2018, p. 23

Levy, M. and Farah Mendlesohn, (2016), *Children's Fantasy Literature: An Introduction*, Cambridge University Press: Cambridge

Lowry, Elizabeth, (2017), Review of *Modern Gods* by Nick Laird in *The Guardian*, 8 July 2018

Maine, David, (2007), *Tall Tales* at www.jewishbookweek.com/2007/270207d.php. Accessed 25 June 2012

Marshall, Donald G., (1995), 'Reading and Interpretive Communities' in *The Discerning Reader: Christian Perspectives on literature and theory*, ed. David Barrett, Roger Pooley and Leland Ryken, Leicester: Inter-Varsity Press

Massie, Alan, (2018), Review of *The Western Wind* by Samantha Harvey in *The Scotsman*, 7 March 2018

McGill, Hannah, (2014), Review of *The Book of Strange New Things* by Michel Faber in *The Independent*, 9 October 2014

McGrath, James F., (2012), *Religion and Science Fiction*, Cambridge: Lutterworth Press

Mendlesohn, Farah, (2003), 'Religion and Science Fiction' in *The Cambridge Companion to Science Fiction*, Cambridge: Cambridge University Press, pp. 264-75

Middleton, Darren J.N., (2008) *Theology after Reading: Christian Imagination and the Power of Fiction*, Waco: Baylor University Press

Mountford, Brian, (2011), *Christian Atheist: Belonging without Believing*, Winchester: O-Books

Neece, Kevin C., (2018), *The Gospel According to Star Trek: The Original Crew*, Cambridge: Lutterworth

Parks, Tim, (2015), *Where I'm Reading From: The Changing World of Books*, London: Vintage Books

Parrinder, Patrick, ed., (1979), *Science Fiction: A Critical Guide*, London: Longman.

Pattison, George, (1998), *The End of Theology – and the Task of Thinking about God*, London: SCM Press

Paul, Robert S., (1991), *Whatever Happened to Sherlock Holmes? Detective Fiction, Popular Theology, and Society*, Carbondale: Southern Illinois University Press

Price, David W., (1999), *History Made, History Imagined: Contemporary Literature, Poesis and the Past*, Champaign: University of Illinois Press

Ratcliffe, Sophie, (2017), 'Copies of the World: Belonging and Belief in Ulster Old and "New"' in *The Times Literary Supplement*, 18 and 25 August 2017

Rayment-Pickard, Hugh, (2004), *The Devil's Account: Philip Pullman and Christianity*, London: Darton Longman and Todd

Roberts, Adam, (2016), *The History of Science Fiction*, Palgrave: London

Rosen, Norma, (1996), *Biblical Women Unbound*, Philadelphia: The Jewish Publication Society

Royce, Josiah, (1968), *The Problem of Christianity*, Chicago: University of Chicago Press

Rushdie, Salman, (1991), *Imaginary Homelands: Essays and Criticism, 1981-1991*, London: Granta

Shortt, Rupert, (2019), *Does Religion Do More Harm Than Good?* London: SPCK

Snyder, Phillip A., (2008), 'Hospitality in Cormac McCarthy's *The Road* in *The Cormac McCarthy Journal* 6 (Autumn 2008)

Stanford, Peter, (2018), Review of *Of Men and Angels* in *The Observer*, 25 March 2018, p. 51

Stephens, Gregory, (2010), 'Feeding Tiger, Finding God: Science, Religion and "the Better Story" in *Life of Pi* in *Intertexts*, Vol. 14 No. 1, pp. 41-59

Storr, Will, (2019), *The Science of Storytelling: Why Stories Make Us Human, and How to Tell Them Better*, London: William Collins

Stratton, Florence, (2004), '"Hollow at the Core": Deconstructing Yann Martel's *Life of Pi* in *Studies in Canadian Literature*, Vol. 29 No. 2, pp. 5-21

Stroup, George W., (1981), *The Promise of Narrative Theology*, London: SCM

Swindell, Anthony C., (2009), *How Contemporary Novelists Rewrite Stories from the Bible*, New York: Edwin Mellen Press

———————, (2010), *Reworking the Bible: The Literary Reception History of Fourteen Biblical Stories*, Sheffield: Sheffield Phoenix Press

Tate, Andrew, (2008), *Contemporary Fiction and Christianity*, London: Continuum.

———————, (2017), 'Predictions of Perilous Times' in *Church Times*, 7 April 2017, p. 22

Templeton, Douglas A., (1999), *The New Testament as True Fiction: Literature, Literary Criticism, Aesthetics*, Sheffield: Sheffield Academic Press

Tew, Philip, (2004), *The Contemporary British Novel*, London: Continuum

Tracy, David, (1981), *The Analogical Imagination: Christian Theology and the Culture of Pluralism*, New York: Crossroad

Vanderheide, John, (2008), 'Sighting Leviathan: Ritualism, Daemonism and the Book of Job in McCarthy's Latest Works' in *Cormac McCarthy Journal*

Wallace, Jennifer, (2008), 'Sarajevo Codex' in *Times Literary Supplement*, 22 February 2008, p. 20

Ward, Graham, (2003), *True Religion*, Oxford: Blackwell

Ward, Keith, (2010), *The Word of God: The Bible after Modern Scholarship*, London: SPCK

Warnes, Christopher, (2005), 'Naturalising the Supernatural: Faith, Irreverence and Magical Realism' in *Literature Compass 2* 20C, no. 106: pp. 5-6

Wielenberg, Erik, J., (2010), 'God, Morality, and Meaning in Cormac McCarthy's *The Road* in *Cormac McCarthy Journal*, Fall 2010

Willey, Basil, (1949), 'Imagination and Fancy' in *Nineteenth Century Studies: Coleridge to Matthew Arnold*, New York: Columbia University Press

Wood, James, (2000), *The Broken Estate: Essays on Literature and Belief*, London: Pimlico

Wright, Terry R., (1988), *Theology and Literature*, Oxford: Basil Blackwell

———————, (2007), *The Genesis of Fiction: Modern Novelists as Biblical Interpreters*, London: Ashgate

Zamora, Lois and Wendy B. Faris, (1995), *Magical Realism: Theory, History, Community*, London: Duke University Press

Index

BV - #0018 - 310120 - C0 - 234/156/9 - PB - 9780718895471